MW00943350

RIBBON OF DARKNESS

America's Broken Covenant

REV. MEL JOLLEY

Bible Scriptures NIV: Scripture quotations marked (NIV) are taken
from the Holy Bible, New International Version®, NIV®. Copyright
© 1973, 1978, 1984, 2011 by Biblica, Inc.™ Used by permission of
Zondervan. All rights reserved worldwide. www.zondervan.com The
"NIV" and "New International Version" are trademarks registered in
the United States Patent and Trademark Office by Biblica, Inc.

Scripture quotations taken from the New American Standard Bible®
(NASB), Copyright © 1960, 1962, 1963, 1968, 1971, 1972, 1973, 1975,
1977, 1995 by The Lockman Foundation Used by permission.

Scripture taken from the King James Version of the Bible.

Scripture taken from the New King James Version®. Copyright © 1982
by Thomas Nelson. Used by permission. All rights reserved.

Archway Publishing books may be ordered through booksellers or by contacting:

Archway Publishing
1663 Liberty Drive
Bloomington, IN 47403
www.archwaypublishing.com
1 (888) 242-5904

Because of the dynamic nature of the Internet, any web addresses or
links contained in this book may have changed since publication and
may no longer be valid. The views expressed in this work are solely those
of the author and do not necessarily reflect the views of the publisher,
and the publisher hereby disclaims any responsibility for them.

Any people depicted in stock imagery provided by Getty Images are
models, and such images are being used for illustrative purposes only.
Certain stock imagery © Getty Images.

ISBN: 978-1-4808-7325-4 (sc)
ISBN: 978-1-4808-7324-7 (e)

Library of Congress Control Number: 2018914726

Print information available on the last page.

Archway Publishing rev. date: 12/27/2018

Dedicated to my Lord God and Savior, Jesus Christ who has created me to glorify Him!

Jude 1:24-25, NIV

"To Him who is able to keep you from stumbling and to present you before His glorious presence without fault and with great joy— [25] to the only God our Savior be glory, majesty, power and authority, through Jesus Christ our Lord, before all ages, now and forevermore! Amen".

1 John 3:16, NIV

"[16] This is how we know what love is: Jesus Christ laid down His life for us. And we ought to lay down our lives for our brothers and sisters".

Contents

CREDITS

I want to take this opportunity to thank Carole, my wife, for all her hard labor, work and talent that she has put into these many years of maintaining my Facebook and YouTube sites for our ministry. I would not be able to do it without her. I have absolutely no computer skills and she is truly a gift from God to me in so many ways.

Thank you to Brother Anthony for his information contributed on Ezekiel 38 and 39. He is an expert in this field and we appreciate his help.

Thank you to our dear friend and sister in the Lord, Nancy. Her time, opinions and help with editing have been very valuable to the creation of this book.

Thank you to Brother Dean who is my mentor and dear friend in the Lord for giving me constructive ideas and advice.

I want to express my gratitude to people like Glenn Beck, and many others, who have stepped up to the plate and continuously, take it on the chin for those of us, who want to be true American citizens. I know many people out there discount him because of his choice of denomination. I want to be clear that I am not so small minded, that I personally let that stand in my way! I think he has proven himself beyond anyone. He stands for principles and integrity. He has given himself and has sacrificed his family in ways that we cannot relate to. He teaches history, such as the serials offered on the Blaze.com, with various subjects on liberals and progressives for those who want to learn why our nation is falling apart. His fruit shows that he puts God first. My prayers go to Glenn and all those who display this kind of courage.

INTRODUCTION

Faith for me grows through hardships, trials and tribulations. When those weeds of life must be pulled out by the roots, and the dead wood is pruned from my flesh, yet I can still rejoice in the Lord! With this faith being nurtured, and watered by the Word of God and like-minded people in Christ, who have the same inalienable rights that He has given and loved me with, I find faith to be my "Miracle Grow" in my Savior.

Father, please remove the scales from our eyes so that we will see the truth of your word as individuals, to fulfill your promises. Amen.

It is my hope that the message I share is a message of finding one's self and building themselves through the Word of Jesus Christ. May we all build a new life as a new creature and have hope in restoring our lives, family and nation to God. I truly believe the only answer to man's problems is found in our Lord's Word.

Before we read any further, I must tell my readers to keep a Bible by you as you read this book, as I refer to the Bible throughout. Many of these entries have happened in the past, such as in the chapter, Presidential Election. In these sections, you will see how some of my thoughts changed as time moves on.

I want my readers to understand, I don't have Face Book and YouTube sites for a popularity test, or to see how many friends I can get. It is not my purpose to tell you what your "itching ears" want to hear in this book. My wish and prayer is to bring the application of God's Word to our everyday lives and current events. This is the only way we can have sanity, serenity and peace amongst ourselves.

2Timmothy 4:3 (New American Standard Bible), "For the time will come when they will not endure sound doctrine; but wanting to have their ears tickled, they will accumulate for themselves teachers in accordance to their own desires".

1 Corinthians 13:1, "If I speak in the tongues of men or of angels, but do not have love, I am only a resounding gong or a clanging cymbal".

In order to have the willingness to change to be Christ like, you must have discipline as well as love. My point is to share this because of the anger people have displayed over Face book, and their willingness to "unfriend" someone who is willing to help and encourage them to do their own investigative work to seek the truth. I am very pleased to see the willingness and the faithfulness from many of you, to seek the truth and have like minds in God's Word, but yet be able to have differences.

CHAPTER ONE
The Holy Spirit

Bob Dylan, who is one of the most prolific writers of our time, wrote a very special song that I like. It is **"Blowing in the wind"**. For those who are believers in Christ, you know that the dove is a symbol of the Holy Spirit as well as the wind. I want to share a few scriptures with you. Read **John 3:5-8.** In this passage, Jesus said unless one is born of water and the Spirit, he cannot enter the kingdom of God. That which is born of the flesh is flesh, and that which is born of the Spirit is spirit. Do not marvel that I said to you, 'You must be born again.' The wind blows where it wishes, and you hear its sound, but you do not know where it comes from or where it goes. So it is with everyone who is born of the Spirit.

John 3:8 NIV, "The wind blows wherever it pleases. You hear its sound, but you cannot tell where it comes from or where it is going. So it is with everyone born of the Spirit." To expound on this thought, I will say that the spirit and the wind are similar in the fact that they are both invisible. You cannot see them, but you see the evidence of them working! For instance, you can feel and see the wind blowing through your hair and across your face. You don't see the wind, but your hair moves across your face and this is the evidence that the wind is blowing and moving! The wind can be felt but yet not seen. The spirit is the Holy Wind of God! You can see the evidence of the spirit moving in a person's life when you see them changing their lives for the good; and when they truly make that change for God and become Christ like!

Please read **Acts 2:1-47.** When the day of Pentecost arrived, they were all together in one place. Suddenly there came a huge sound like a mighty wind, rushing throughout the entire house where they were sitting. Divided tongues of fire appeared to them and rested on each one. As they were all filled with the Holy Spirit and began to speak in other tongues, the Spirit moved upon them and gave utterance to them. Now there were dwelling in Jerusalem Jews, and devout men from every nation and all were amazed that these who spoke were not all Galileans. They heard in their own individual languages! As you read and then listen to the words of Bob Dylan's song, let those who have an ear, hear the word of God.

Two Covenants

Abraham and Sarah

My purpose is to enhance the knowledge and wisdom of those who choose to follow the Lord. Here is some general information to help you understand the news and current events of today and how they relate to the Bible. It started when Abram was promised by God to be the "Father of many nations". His name was changed to Abraham by God Himself. God also changed Sarai's name to Sarah at that time. Now Sarah was barren and was too old to conceive. Her child bearing years were well over. In an effort to make the prophecy come true, Sarah tried to "help" by offering her handmaid, Hagar to bear a child for her. Abraham, being an "obedient husband" obliged Sarah. As a result, Ishmael was born. He was not the promised son from God. The promise was to Abraham and his wife Sarah from whom the promised son would be born about fourteen years later. Sarah was 90 and Abraham was 100 years old. So now we have two sons, Ishmael and Isaac. Ishmael was the son of the flesh, man's way, the world's way, and Isaac was the <u>promised son</u> in which the Messiah, the son of

God would come. This is why Christians and Jews say "we serve the God of Abraham, Isaac, and Jacob" as opposed to saying the "God of Abraham, Ishmael and his sons". Please continue following with me as we see how "deception", "progressiveness", and "liberalism" bring consequences by not following God's Word.

Isaac, Esau, and Jacob

Isaac was the father of Esau and Jacob. The Book of Genesis speaks of the relationship between Jacob and Esau, focusing on Esau's loss of his birthright to Jacob! This spawned conflict between their descendant nations. Because of Jacob's deception, Isaac, received Esau's birthright and blessing. From conception, their conflict was foreshadowed, when the children struggled together within Rebecca; she asked the Lord, "why is this happening"? And the Lord said to her, "two nations are in your womb, and two manners of people; and the one people shall be stronger than the other people; and the elder shall serve the younger." This passage is explained in Genesis 25:26. It is as if Jacob were trying to pull Esau back into the womb so that he could be firstborn. The grasping of the heel is also a reference to deceptive behavior. This conflict was paralleled by the affection the parents had for their favored child: Isaac loved Esau, because he was a hunter, and Rebekah loved Jacob because he had God's favor.

Jacob

Jacob, later given the name Israel, is regarded as a Patriarch of the Israelites. He is the son of Isaac and

Rebecca, the grandson of Abraham and Sarah. Jacob had twelve sons and at least one daughter, by his two wives, Leah and Rachel, and by their handmaidens, Bilhah and Zilpah. Jacob's twelve sons, named in Genesis, were Reuben, Simeon, Levi, Judah, Dan, Naphtali, Gad, Asher, Issachar, Zebulun, Joseph, and Benjamin. His daughter mentioned in Genesis is Dinah. The twelve sons became the "Twelve Tribes".

Joseph

From a young age Joseph had visions that caused his brothers to become very jealous and resentful. They decided to sell him to traders and tell their father that he was killed, showing Jacob, the bloody torn coat of many colors. Years later there was a severe drought in Canaan. Jacob and his sons moved to Egypt at the time when his son Joseph was viceroy. After 17 years in Egypt, Jacob died and Joseph carried Jacob's remains to the land of Canaan. Jacob was buried in the Cave of Machpelah along with Abraham, Sarah, Isaac, Rebecca, and Jacob's first wife, Leah.

The Land of Israel

God promised that He would give the land of Israel to the Jewish people as an eternal possession. The promise was unconditional. God confirmed it with an oath and stated that the covenant was everlasting throughout the Bible. Moab is Palestine today. God gave the direct boundary lines to Israel for their home land. He said, "the boundaries of the "Promised Land" shall never change. I will plant Israel in their own land, never again to be uprooted from the land I have given them", Amos 9:15 (NIV).

Please read and refer to Deuteronomy 29 in your Bible. Some 3,500 years ago the Canaanites inhabited the land that God promised to give to the offspring of Abraham, Isaac and Jacob. God did bring the Israelites into the Promised Land forty years after the Exodus from Egypt. Israel reached the peak of her power some 500 years later under King Solomon. The descendants of Ishmael would later follow the Islamic religion and worship Allah. This fact is part of the reason that Islam is playing such an important role in the news right now and will eventually lead to the Christians' anti-Christ, which in turn is the Islamic "Mahdi", or Muslim Messiah.

Moses

We know the holiness of Moses. I find something very interesting about his life. Moses is the one who God made a covenant <u>with</u>. He gave to Moses the commandments, kingdom principles and values. I want us to look at this part of his life which is overlooked very often, and how it applies to our situation today. There are many references to be made to Moses' disobedience which was rooted in anger over the people for their nonbelief. Agreeing to the Word of God and then waffling would inflame Moses to rage. My best advice for us is to pray that the Holy Spirit keep us clear minded and that we shall overcome that rage through God's principles and values and not our flesh.

Regarding Exodus

Please read Duet 4:39-40 in your Bible. For further information read Duet 5 also. Give some thought to this. When God sent Moses to Egypt to set the Israelites free there was some problems along the way. Of all the people who left Egypt with Moses, not all were Israelites and not all were sold out to God. Many of them were murmurers and complainers, crybabies, entitled people with an "all about me" attitude much like todays' progressives and liberals who are always searching for another god or easier way out. Moses loved God so much that their bickering and complaining had an effect on him. Yet God mightily used him. Now I would like you to focus on Pharaoh. You talk about a man who had an attitude and a deviate mind, even after Moses came back to him ten different times through all the plagues and warnings he still refused to see God's truth through Moses. Pharaoh had to pay a price along with the land and people of Egypt. There is undeniable comparison to what is happening in America today, in Glenn Beck's book, "Liars", in which God has revealed much truth and integrity.

The description of Israel promised to Abraham, Isaac and Jacob.

Read Duet 34:1-4 (NIV). The Lord showed Moses the whole land from Gilead to Dan, all of Naphtali, the territory of Ephraim and Manasseh, all of Judah as far as the Mediterranean Sea, The Negev and the whole region of the Valley of Jericho, the city of Palms as far as Zoar. The Lord told Him this is the land He promised on oath to Abraham,

Isaac and Jacob when He promised to give it to Abrahams's descendants. God allowed Moses to see it but because of His disobedience to God in the desert He was not allowed to cross over into the Promised Land.

As you read this remember that The United States comes under a similar covenant and oath as Israel. Our forefathers did the same as Israel. Many may not know the two nations that have a covenant with God. My purpose is to give you an overview and cause you to seek the truth for yourself.

George Washington's Covenant with God

George Washington made a Covenant with God and he gave the very first presidential oath and the very first inaugural address in New York City, the then capital of our nation. God honors covenants. He would always keep His end of the bargain. George Washington knew that. The question is would the United States of America keep hers? It's a matter of public record that George Washington said "I do solemnly swear that I will faithfully execute the Office of the President of the United States, and will to the best of my Ability, preserve, protect and defend the Constitution of the United States. So help me God."

First inaugural address

In George Washington's first inaugural address, he opened with prayer. George Washington made a covenant with God saying: "Since we ought to be no less persuaded that the propitious smiles of Heaven, can never be expected on a nation that disregards the eternal rules of order and right, which Heaven itself has ordained: And since the preservation of the sacred fire of liberty, and the destiny of the Republican model of Government, are justly considered as deeply, perhaps as finally staked, on the experiment entrusted to the hands of the American people".

So in his address we can see that George Washington clearly wanted the nation to be blessed by God and that the blessings from God required obedience to God's Word. If disobedience occurred then the blessing would cease. George Washington made a promise that the United States of America would follow God. If she ever broke her promise then she would lose God's blessings and protection. God keeps His promises and The United States of America has to keep her promises to God for the Covenant to be in effect.

How is George Washington like Moses?

He is likened unto Moses in guiding America into a republic nation through a covenant made with Jesus Christ. Moses led the Israelites to the "promised land" and made a covenant with the God of Israel. George Washington realized the republic could flourish only if it were grounded on religion and morality. These were the "indispensable supports" of "political prosperity" and human happiness. "Virtue or morality," Thomas Jefferson labeled "the fair experiment": Was freedom of religion "compatible with order in government and obedience to the laws"? The First Amendment mandated that the United States could not establish a national church. Could such a nation endure?

If the government did not provide financial and political support for Christianity, would it survive? Our forefathers knew the value of the principles in the Bible such as the "Ten Commandments, Proverbs, and Beatitudes."

Chapter Three
Israel

Jesus, the Jew

I am in love with a Jew, are you?

First He was in love with you and me.

They even wanted to kill Him when He was a baby.

All through His childhood and His life they made fun of Him.

Would you be willing to stand with and support the lover of your soul?

Every time I think of Him going to the cross I start to cry because I know the lies and false accusations they made about Him. They still lie about Him to this day, and even try to steal His identity, all because He loved you and me!

If you know Him like I do, you know that all He wanted was the very best for us. He was always so sincere. He never lied like those who try to govern or rule us. Whenever I am hurting He is always there to help heal my wounds and scars.

He was whipped for you and me so we could be healed. His blood was shed for the remission of our sins. He died and was buried; He descended into hell and on the third day He arose so you and I can have eternal life with Him.

Now He sits upon the right hand of His Father so that we would not have to spend eternity in hell.

Are you in love with the same Jew?

His name is Jesus. He was crucified for me and you.

Written by Rev. Mel Jolley

The description of Israel promised to Abraham, Isaac and Jacob.

As stated in the previous chapter, The Lord showed Moses the whole land from Gilead to Dan, all of Naphtali, the territory of Ephraim and Manasseh, all of Judah as far as the Mediterranean Sea, The Negev and the whole region of the Valley of Jericho, the city of Palms as far as Zoar. The Lord told Him this is the land He promised on oath to Abraham, Isaac and Jacob when He promised to give it to Abrahams's descendants. God promised to give the land of Israel to the Jewish people as an eternal possession. This is very important so it is worth repeating! The promise was unconditional. God confirmed it with an oath and stated that the covenant was everlasting throughout the Bible. Moab is Palestine today. God gave the direct boundary lines to Israel for their home land. He said, "the boundaries of the "Promised Land" shall never change. I will plant Israel in their own land, never again to be uprooted from the land I have given them", Amos 9:15 (NIV).

The Persian Empire

Numerous historic states and many modern countries became part of the Persian Empire, including: Iran, western Afghanistan, western Pakistan, Kuwait, Iraq, northern Saudi Arabia, Jordan, Israel/Palestine, eastern Egypt, Syria, Turkey, and northern Greece. The first empire of Persia was the Achaemenid Empire of Cyrus the Great, which fought with the Greeks and lasted from around 550 BC to 330 BC, when much of its territory was conquered by Alexander the Great. The Seleucid Greek Empire was succeeded in Persia by a smaller dominion known as the Parthian Empire, from 247 BC to 224 AD. This kingdom fell under the rule of Ardashir I of the Fars Province in Persia, who created the Sassanid Empire (also known as the Second Persian Empire), which was mostly confined to SW Asia and lasted from 224 to 651 AD, when it was conquered by Islamic Arabs.

Ezekiel 32:30, King James Bible, "There *be* the princes of the north, all of them, and all the Zidonians, which are gone down with the slain; with their terror they are ashamed of their might; and they lie uncircumcised with *them that be* slain by the sword, and bear their shame with them that go down to the pit."

The wisdom that Netanyahu has for the land of Judah in Israel, as well as the first 4 books of Moses, surely shows the wisdom of this leader. Netanyahu has a clear understanding of the boundaries that the God of Abraham, Isaac, and Jacob has given to Israel. He has the wisdom to know when to go into battle. He surely knows that the Hand of his God will be with him and his nation. God has ordained His people and their land, who call Him by His name, to go into battle for they will be preserved and protected.

CHAPTER FOUR
The Founders

Pilgrims

History tells us that the Pilgrims were Europeans and came to America for the main reason of wanting freedom of religion and church. They did not want a state led church. They settled in Plymouth Colony in Massachusetts. While they were aboard the May- Flower through much discussion amongst themselves they made the Mayflower com- pact. They brought with them the Geneva Bible. The Geneva Bible is one of the most historically significant translations of the Bible into English, preceding the King James Version by 51 years. These were people of strong principles and values as well as people of strong faith in God in seeking a new land for Christ where they could have the freedom of practicing their faith in God. They were all under the King's Church of England and held Puritan Calvinist religious beliefs but, unlike other Puritans, they maintained that their congregations needed to be separated from the English State Church. The Mayflower Compact, signed by 41 English colonists on the ship Mayflower on November 11, 1620, was the first written form of government established in the United States. The compact was drafted to prevent disagreements and differences of opinion amongst Puritans and non-separatist Pilgrims who had landed at Plymouth a few days earlier.

For me, I am thankful for the Pilgrims and Colonists who were seeking freedom. This nation was founded on common principles and values through the Word of God and His promises so that all people can agree. They no longer wanted tyranny but they wanted liberty for all. The common denominator that they had was founded in the Bible. It is my prayer as long as there is breath in my body that God would use me to continue to bring these truths to the people of this world and America. The Colonist had to learn to be independent and productive in order to survive. Through these common things America's growth gave birth to the Constitution and the Bill of Rights. The deterioration is in the people who want to revise these articles which weaken our foundation and Christian-Judeo principles and the values that made us strong. We come to realize that the truth is a "God matter" that we cannot live without Christ being our guiding light. As we drift away from Him we just don't destroy ourselves and family, but we bring down our nation and the world. This is why the Bible says: **2 Timothy 2:15 (KJV),**"15 Study to shew thyself approved unto God, a workman that needeth not to be ashamed, rightly dividing the word of truth."

Breaking the Convenant

When we take God out of the school system you see the breaking of the covenant that America made. In colonial America, everyone with schooling knew one book thoroughly: the Bible. The Old Testament mattered as much as the New, for the American colonies were founded in a time of renewed Hebrew scholarship, and the Calvinistic character of Christian faith in early America emphasized the legacy of Israel. The Bible indeed was the first textbook followed by the New England Primer popular in the 1700 and 1800's.

We the people must carry the light of liberty. It is not going to happen in the majority of the churches or schools in America. Independence Day is not about drugging or getting drunk. It is not about how many dollars we can blow up in fireworks. It is not about how many hamburgers or hot dogs we can stuff down our gullets. Perhaps the next 4th of July you will see it's up to us by having Bible studies, or reading groups to teach ourselves and others of the true American heritage in history. You will find most of our leaders do not have an understanding of the Declaration of Independence or its true meaning or where its roots came from. The same is to be said about the Constitution. It would behoove us to accomplish what the church refuses to do because of its inaccurate stand on separation of state and government.

The Declaration of Independence: A Transcription

IN CONGRESS, July 4, 1776.

The unanimous Declaration of the thirteen united States of America,

When in the Course of human events, it becomes necessary for one people to dissolve the political bands which have connected them with another, and to assume among the powers of the earth, the separate and equal station to which the Laws of Nature and of Nature's God entitle them, a decent respect to the opinions of mankind requires that they should declare the causes which impel them to the separation.

We hold these truths to be self-evident, that all men are created equal, that they are endowed by their Creator with certain unalienable Rights, that among these are Life, Liberty and the pursuit of Happiness.—That to secure these rights, Governments are instituted among Men, deriving their just powers from the consent of the governed, —That whenever any Form of Government becomes destructive of these ends, it is the Right of the People to alter or to abolish it, and to institute new Government, laying its foundation on such principles and organizing its powers in such form, as to them shall seem most likely to effect their Safety and Happiness. Prudence, indeed, will dictate that Governments long established should not be changed for light and transient causes; and accordingly all experience hath shewn, that mankind are more disposed to suffer, while evils are sufferable, than to right themselves by abolishing the forms to which they are accustomed. But when a long train of abuses and usurpations, pursuing invariably the same Object evinces a design to reduce them under absolute Despotism, it is their right, it is their duty, to throw off such Government, and to provide new

Guards for their future security.—Such has been the patient sufferance of these Colonies; and such is now the necessity which constrains them to alter their former Systems of Government. The history of the present King of Great Britain is a history of repeated injuries and usurpations, all having in direct object the establishment of an absolute Tyranny over these States. To prove this, let Facts be submitted to a candid world.

He has refused his Assent to Laws, the most wholesome and necessary for the public good.

He has forbidden his Governors to pass Laws of immediate and pressing importance, unless suspended in their operation till his Assent should be obtained; and when so suspended, he has utterly neglected to attend to them.

He has refused to pass other Laws for the accommodation of large districts of people, unless those people would relinquish the right of Representation in the Legislature, a right inestimable to them and formidable to tyrants only.

He has called together legislative bodies at places unusual, uncomfortable, and distant from the depository of their public Records, for the sole purpose of fatiguing them into compliance with his measures.

He has dissolved Representative Houses repeatedly, for opposing with manly firmness his invasions on the rights of the people.

He has refused for a long time, after such dissolutions, to cause others to be elected; whereby the Legislative powers, incapable of Annihilation, have returned to the People at large for their exercise; the State remaining in the mean time exposed to all the dangers of invasion from without, and convulsions within.

He has endeavoured to prevent the population of these States; for that purpose obstructing the Laws for Naturalization of Foreigners; refusing to pass others to encourage their migrations hither, and raising the conditions of new Appropriations of Lands.

He has obstructed the Administration of Justice, by refusing his Assent to Laws for establishing Judiciary powers.

He has made Judges dependent on his Will alone, for the tenure of their offices, and the amount and payment of their salaries.

He has erected a multitude of New Offices, and sent hither swarms of Officers to harrass our people, and eat out their substance.

He has kept among us, in times of peace, Standing Armies without the Consent of our legislatures.

He has affected to render the Military independent of and superior to the Civil power.

He has combined with others to subject us to a jurisdiction foreign to our constitution, and unacknowledged by our laws; giving his Assent to their Acts of pretended Legislation:

For Quartering large bodies of armed troops among us:

For protecting them, by a mock Trial, from punishment for any Murders which they should commit on the Inhabitants of these States:

For cutting off our Trade with all parts of the world:

For imposing Taxes on us without our Consent:

For depriving us in many cases, of the benefits of Trial by Jury:

For transporting us beyond Seas to be tried for pretended offences

For abolishing the free System of English Laws in a neighbouring Province, establishing therein an Arbitrary government, and enlarging its Boundaries so as to render it at once an example and fit instrument for introducing the same absolute rule into these Colonies:

For taking away our Charters, abolishing our most valuable Laws, and altering fundamentally the Forms of our Governments:

For suspending our own Legislatures, and declaring themselves invested with power to legislate for us in all cases whatsoever.

He has abdicated Government here, by declaring us out of his Protection and waging War against us.

He has plundered our seas, ravaged our Coasts, burnt our towns, and destroyed the lives of our people.

He is at this time transporting large Armies of foreign Mercenaries to compleat the works of death, desolation and tyranny, already begun with circumstances of Cruelty & perfidy scarcely paralleled in the most barbarous ages, and totally unworthy the Head of a civilized nation.

He has constrained our fellow Citizens taken Captive on the high Seas to bear Arms against their Country, to become the executioners of their friends and Brethren, or to fall themselves by their Hands.

He has excited domestic insurrections amongst us, and has endeavoured to bring on the inhabitants of our frontiers, the merciless Indian Savages, whose known rule of warfare, is an undistinguished destruction of all ages, sexes and conditions.

In every stage of these Oppressions We have Petitioned for Redress in the most humble terms: Our repeated Petitions have been answered only by repeated injury. A Prince whose character is thus marked by every act which may define a Tyrant, is unfit to be the ruler of a free people.

Nor have We been wanting in attentions to our Brittish brethren. We have warned them from time to time of attempts by their legislature to extend an unwarrantable jurisdiction over us. We have reminded them of the circumstances of our emigration and settlement here. We have appealed to their native justice and magnanimity, and we have conjured them by the ties of our common kindred to disavow these usurpations, which, would inevitably interrupt our connections and correspondence. They too have been deaf to the voice of justice and of consanguinity. We must, therefore, acquiesce in the necessity, which denounces our Separation, and hold them, as we hold the rest of mankind, Enemies in War, in Peace Friends.

We, therefore, the Representatives of the united States of America, in General Congress, Assembled, appealing to the Supreme Judge of the world for the rectitude of our intentions, do, in the Name, and by Authority of the good People of these Colonies, solemnly publish and declare, That these United Colonies are, and of Right ought to be Free and Independent States; that they are Absolved from all Allegiance to the British Crown, and that all political connection between them and the State

of Great Britain, is and ought to be totally dissolved; and that as Free and Independent States, they have full Power to levy War, conclude Peace, contract Alliances, establish Commerce, and to do all other Acts and Things which Independent States may of right do. And for the support of this Declaration, with a firm reliance on the protection of divine Providence, we mutually pledge to each other our Lives, our Fortunes and our sacred Honor.

It would seem to me that if we love God as we love the church that we would love our nation and the dream that our founders entrusted to us. There are many books out there to teach us how our Constitution, Bill of Rights, and government came into existence and are supported scripturally along with the Bible. There are books that will teach us about liberals, progressives, socialists, as well as Marxists and communists. These books can be used alongside the Bible. It's good for us to have an understanding of our inalienable rights which were given to us directly by God. Our founders understood these principles and values when they set up the Judeo-Christian government. With this knowledge we will be able to vote with the knowledge of knowing what is of God and what isn't. We will be able to fight this war against evil righteously and with a pure heart. We will be able to confront the enemy with power that cannot be argued with. That is why it is important for us to understand our Judeo-Christian principles and heritage biblically. I will give you a list of suggested books that you can supply yourself with for Bible studies.

The 5000 year Leap, by Dr. W. Cleon Skousen. This has a complete study guide and kit. DVDs are available for it.

"Building of America", by David Barton, through Wallbuilders.com.

"The Righteous mind", by Jonthan Haidt.

People should start study groups in their homes across this nation to prepare themselves in the direction to vote and also who not to vote for!

God's Principles and Values

Christians who want their freedoms and liberties must desire God's principles and values, which came to our government through a covenant with God through our founders. God has been warning the Christian people for a number of years now that we must act and fight for what we want. It's critical that we choose Jesus Christ or make the decision to follow the anti-Christ. These are the options that it has come down to. The time of not taking things seriously is over. It's no longer a cat and mouse game. Every time we vote, speak and respond, we have to do it in the way of the Lord. Sin is sin and is not of Christ. We must wash our hands clean of those who refuse to serve our nation by the word of God with God's principles. If your church is not active, seek one that is. Be active and stand for righteousness along with God's principles and values.

CHAPTER FIVE
The Black Robe Regiment

Read 2 Timothy 2:2-4. This passage says the things that you have heard of me from many witnesses, commit to faithful men, who will be able to teach to others also. Be a good soldier of Jesus Christ and endure hardness. No man of war worries about anything other than pleasing his authorities who have chosen him to be a soldier. We must think of ourselves as warriors for Christ. All warriors are prepared to be persecuted and lay down their lives. We must teach and instruct the things that we have learned to others, who will teach and instruct still others and become warriors for Christ. Therefore you must be prepared by enduring hard things that come to you in life. If you are a warrior, Christ must be first in your life. You cannot be entangled in the things of this world, but rather your goal must be to please the Lord who has chosen you to be His soldier.

A Soldier of God

Somewhere out there on the battle field it seems there is a soldier of God who perhaps has fallen. As he reaches out with tears in his eyes, and cheeks like dew on the roses as they spread to his lips as sweet as honey in the comb. The ground beneath his face grows damp with his tears, his arms that are so long and powerful surround him and comfort him with those principles and moral values that came from his lips. Only the sweet comfort of the Spirit of God brings this serenity and comfort home again.

Written by Rev. Mel Jolley

What is the Black Robe Regiment?

The Black Robe Regiment is a resource and networking entity where church leaders and laypeople can network and educate themselves as to our biblical responsibility to stand up for our Lord and Savior and to protect the freedoms and liberties granted to a moral people in the divinely inspired US Constitution. The Regiment had its historical beginnings during the Revolutionary War when Pastors from across the colonies arose and lead their congregations into the battle for freedom. Unlike today, the church during this time served as the center-point for political debate and discussion on the relevant news of the day. Today's church leaders have all but lost that concept of leading their congregations in a Godly manner in all aspects of their worldly existence and are afraid to speak out against the progressive agenda that has dominated our political system for the past century. Through this time the church and God Himself has been under assault by the progressives and secularists. The false wall of separation of church and state has been constructed in such a manner that most are unaware of its limited boundaries. The church and the body of Christ has been attacked on all fronts and challenged by the progressive courts and groups such as the ACLU while we have sat idle in consent.

About the Black Robe Regiment

The Black Robe Regiment represents a group of pulpit ministers who were extremely active during the American Revolution. Much of the news of the day was obtained in the pulpits of the churches. It was this group of individuals from the pulpit who assisted in inspiring the souls and hearts of the men and women during that time to gather in defense of a society which was being tyrannized by a despotic government that was creating an environment where freedom and liberty would no longer exist.

The Black Robe Regiment began in 1776 when Pastor Muhlenberg preached from Ecclesiastes 3. Please refer to Ecclesiastes 3 in your Bible. This is the "season for every purpose" passage. After his sermon he removed his pastoral robe and he was dressed in a military uniform. He went to the back of the church and asked his congregation, "Who is willing to join me in fighting for our liberty?" This was the beginning of the 8th Virginia Brigade. It is public record that Pastor Muhlenberg said "I am a Clergyman it is true, but I am a member of the Society as well as the poorest Layman, and my Liberty is as dear to me as any man, shall I then sit still and enjoy myself at home, when the best Blood of the Covenant is spilling? ...So far am I from thinking that I act wrong, I am convinced it is my duty to do so and duly I owe to God and my country."

The above is one story of one pastor who chose the path of Liberty and Freedom. That Liberty and Freedom has been graciously bestowed by our Heavenly Father to each of us. It has been freely offered, freely sacrificed for by Jesus Christ and it is the duty of each of us to acknowledge that precious gift and to not give it away lightly. There were hundreds of such men and women during that period of American History who chose the path that Pastor Muhlenberg took. There were many such brave souls who opted to sacrifice all for "God, Family, and Country" during that period of the birth of our nation and during other such battles as these, before and after this Revolution. What America is now becoming is not what the Creator envisioned or created, nor what our forefathers and mothers hoped to realize. It is not at all what they bled and died for.

The pastors of that day, and their congregations, were living out of what had come over a 100 year period. Religion and politics were combined together. There was no separation between the two spheres. This Revolution against Britain would create a totally different awareness and way of life than had ever been lived before; a <u>Republic</u> form of government with a hope and a promise. The people had an awareness that the people who inhabited this country had to be a moral and upright people; people who followed Christian –Judeo principles. The early Americans felt it was a "New Jerusalem". A New Eden that Christopher Columbus saw, and was living out what they saw as a life and a country that was fashioned entirely by their Creator. The Constitution and the Declaration of Independence were and are a covenant between the people of America and God. It was written for a Christian-Judeo people who are fully able to internally govern themselves; thus, the meaning of a

Republic that was inspired by God's Word. America was to be that city or nation on a Hill, and be the mission of God's children and Christ's ambassadors to reach out to the Earth.

Each of us has inherited in some form, the genetic material of these people who came seeking Liberty and Justice. These people endured severe hardships from their countries of origin, despotic rule that came in the form of religious, political, and educational structure.

Christians, when they have lived up to the highest ideals of their faith, have defended the weak and vulnerable and worked tirelessly to protect and strengthen vital institutions of civil society, beginning with the family. It was in this tradition that a group of prominent Christian clergy, ministry leaders, and scholars released the "Manhattan Declaration" on November 20, 2009 at a press conference in Washington, DC. The declaration speaks in defense of the sanctity of life, traditional marriage, and religious liberty. It summons an urgent call to Christians to adhere firmly to their convictions in these three areas. The Manhattan Declaration has been signed by people all over the United States who are standing arm in arm and speaking in a clear and united voice in defense of life, marriage, and religious liberty.

GET INVOLVED!

Become part of the growing grassroots movement of people taking a principled stand on the three critical moral issues of our time: The sanctity of human life, the dignity of traditional marriage, and religious liberty!

The time has come that we must now arise and

awaken to the danger of this hyper-progressive agenda that so permeates every aspect of our political, legal, and educational systems. It is time now to educate ourselves and push back against the erosion of our freedoms and liberties and restore the constitutional authority back to all aspects of our government with its original intent. It will take the leaders of our churches to shepherd their flocks as did our forefathers during our first fight for liberty.

The Black Robe Regiment is to serve as a resource and reference for church leaders and laypeople. It is to be a portal for Christians to communicate and network in order to restore the body of Christ to its rightful position of tolerant leadership in all aspects of our government. We all need to learn the Constitution! One of the most important things that we as Americans can do is to inform ourselves. We need to learn about how the Founding Fathers derived the near perfect balance of government in the US Constitution, and how the balance has been shifted over the course of time, which is a lesson we must all understand. The National Center for Constitutional Studies is a great place to start. They offer numerous resources and can also provide training classes at your church.

About the National Center for Constitutional Studies:

The National Center for Constitutional Studies is a nonprofit educational foundation created to teach the U.S. Constitution in the tradition of America's Founding Fathers. It was founded in 1971 by Dr. W. Cleon Skousen. The NCCS has taught throughout America the original principles and ideas drafted by our Founding Fathers over

220 years ago whose purpose is to help build the culture of liberty and union which the Founders sought to secure for them and their posterity. America and its Constitution were established by the hand of God; and thus we must advocate morality and religious principles as the essential foundation of human happiness and freedom.

CHAPTER SIX

Who is an American?

First Americans

A true American was a person who came from a foreign nation as an immigrant to America in hopes of finding freedom and liberty which they could not find in their own home land. They were seeking prosperity for themselves to fulfill their visions and dreams. Over the years, these immigrants have come here to attain these freedoms without destroying the idea of what America is. America was founded on Christian- Judeo principles and values, not that of other foreign gods. I believe that it is time for all God's children, "those who seek Christ in all things", to continue fighting this battle against evil coming in and destroying our nations' heritage.

If we are Americans we need a clear understanding that Jesus Christ is our foundation and our God. Christian -Judeo principles formed this nation from the very beginning. We also need a firm understanding of the American documents, the Constitution, Declaration of Independence, and the Bill of Rights. They do not need to be changed, but they need to be restored in our political and justice systems, as well as in our public, and private schools. As you can see from watching the news and reading newspapers, it is plain to see that our media as well as our political officials are not willing to uphold the laws of America themselves. Therefore it causes great chaos with our justice system, as well as the Church, because of blatant ignorance and refusal to stand for what is righteousness, with godly principles and values given to us by our forefathers. This chaos has prevented us from running a fair nation with "liberty and freedom for all".

Ignorance of the law is of no excuse. You have the freedom of religion in America. Sharia Law has no place in America, and does not work with American law, which is based on Christian- Judeo principles, which totally oppose Sharia Law. Foreign religions do not have the right to come into America and over- shadow and discriminate to take away the right of the Christian's belief that our nation was founded and built upon. Allah, Mohamed, Krishna, Buddha, and others did not give us our Constitution, liberties or freedoms. It would do us good to search back and see what God's Word says about this, especially when it comes to Islam. I refer you to these websites: Shamram Hadion, (http://www.tilproject.com/) and also Wallid Shoebat, http://shoebat.com/)

People have asked me how the principles and values apply to the judiciary branch of the government. For good information on this, start with the Bible. The Levitical laws were given to Moses on how to run a family as well as a nation. You will find this in Leviticus, Chapters 18-20. I would also encourage you to get the book, <u>Building of</u>

<u>America,</u> through Wall Builders.com. It will be very clear to you on how America was formed and how the judiciary, "Levitical", law has become corrupt through the years by the liberals and progressive minds.

American people better start worrying about Alexander Dugan, Putin, along with Alex Jones, Bill and Hilary Clinton, and the effect that they are having on America and its citizens and the church. Putin with Alexander Dugan are being very successful at dividing the people in America with hate and discontentment. I advise you to learn more about them.

What standard does a person go by to consider themselves a Christian?

As I think about these things I am more aware that America truly is not America any longer. We don't go by Biblical standards that the God of Abraham, Isaac and Jacob set before us. We don't go by the standards that the pilgrims and puritans brought to us, or the Constitution and Bill of Rights that our forefathers brought to us. Just what do we hold sacred, pure, and righteous any longer? It certainly isn't life when we are clamoring to throw un- born children in the trash or flush them down the toilet and the government is willing to go with euthanasia to eliminate the seniors and disabled as well as the undesirables or terminally ill. It certainly isn't our moral values when we see all of our heroes and government officials as well as super stars embracing immorality whenever and wherever. We are willing to entice the youth with illegal drugs by legalizing them and providing "safe drug houses". We no longer know the truth when we hear it. We live in a time when a lie is the truth, dishonesty is acceptable. Has America always been this way? Or is it just me? It makes me wonder why we celebrate our Saviors birth at Christmas?

CHAPTER SEVEN
False gods

Abba Jehova,

I intercede for my brothers and sisters who find it hard to lay their flesh down and let it die. They cling to their wickedness and refuse to lift their hands towards heaven and allow the anointing of God to flow down their hands over their head to cleanse their minds and spirit. I truly understand what my brother Paul, in Christ, was saying that one must die to themselves to inherit the kingdom of heaven. It grieves me that there are those who proclaim to be my brothers and sisters, but they are not, because they reject the words of their Messiah. They do not see the fire in your eyes Lord, or the breast plate of righteousness. They refuse the bread of life; they actually seek after the god of this world and believe in his evil and lies. They actually turn on me as a serpent, and strike out at your holiness, Lord, rather than lay themselves up on the altar of eternal life and cleanse themselves by the blood you shed at Calvary.
Written by Rev. Mel Jolley

1 Thessalonians 1:9-10 (New American Standard Bible), "⁹ For they themselves report about us what kind of a reception we had with you, and how you turned to God from idols to serve a living and true God, ¹⁰ and to wait for His Son from heaven, whom He raised from the dead, *that is* Jesus, who rescues us from the wrath to come".

False Teaching

We all need to be aware of this. This is happening big time now. There is a lot of false teaching out there on how to get to heaven. It's made its way into many of our churches. There are people who are lying vipers spreading a poisoness gospel, saying that there are many ways to God and heaven other than "Jesus is the only way." They are mixing New Age with Chrislam and disguising it as gospel. Oprah Winfrey, who came from a Baptist background, Pastor Rob Bell, Rick Warren from the Saddleback Church, and Dr. Oz to name a few. There are many others as well, who are willing and trying to bring on a phony spiritual awakening, which is anti-Christ. Be not deceived! Be diligent and watch for this creeping into your church body. This is why we need to educate ourselves and read, read, read the Bible! Don't let a day go by without reading and studying the scripture. If you know the scriptures you won't be deceived.

These are perilous times! When we the people keep voting for immorality, legalizing sin and corruption; when we allow people who commit treason, and support our enemies, and have no moral values to be candidates and run for office. All the time we are willing to point the finger at somebody else, badger them, and spread malicious gossip, while we are not ready to be accountable ourselves; to the point of having the willingness to change our life styles. We are to believe that the person who chooses to follow Christ has no right to fight for their inalienable rights. All the while we vote for other gods to kneel to and are expected to accept them above the one true God. We are totally destroying ourselves from within by not submitting ourselves to the Word of God. There is no double standard in God's Kingdom!

It seems to me our founders were more knowledgeable about the Bible than we are today. Maybe we ought to proclaim a "national soap dish day" for those who choose and legalize Sharia law in their county, city, state, and nation. That surly will bring the hand of wrath upon the people. God is a jealous God for there are no other gods before Him as stated in the Ten Commandments. Every knee shall bow and every tongue will confess that Jesus Christ is Lord. If we the people don't change our morals, principle values, and live the way God intended us to live, than it really doesn't matter how you vote. You will get what you deserve.

Easter or Resurrection Sunday?

Speaking frankly now, it occurred to me last night in our Monday night Bible Study in Deuteronomy: Chapter 22, just how far we have fallen into deception. I'm sure for the majority of people it's beyond no return. You probably might be asking why? My answer is not going to be very pleasing to many, but I believe it to be the truth. That is, one word, phonies! Phonies have taken over the church! What in the world is the church doing talking about Easter and Resurrection Sunday in the same sentence? We are not to be serving two gods. You cannot be blessed by God through Jesus Christ and recognize Easter. Easter is the worship of the goddess Eostre. She was the Great Mother Goddess of the Saxon people in Northern Europe. How many of us are actually focused on the true meaning of the resurrection power of Jesus Christ? What does the goddess Estra or Eostre, have to do with the resurrection power of Jesus Christ? There is scientific proof that the shroud of Torren has a miraculous photo print of Jesus Christ's body. It was caused from the resurrection power when He arose from the tomb. We know that particular tomb where His body was laid, is now empty. There is substantial scientific evidence that the resurrection power of Jesus Christ still affects all of creation. Many have proclaimed as well as testified about healing and people coming back from the dead; being resurrected!

I would like for you to take the time to look at the resurrection story in the Book of Luke and also when Christ committed His spirit into His Father's hands. You will see the super natural power that was displayed at these given times. I would like you to look at what happens when the Messiah returns. Zechariah 14:4 (NIV), "On that day His feet will stand on the Mount of Olives, east of Jerusalem, and the Mount of Olives will be split in two from east to west, forming a great valley, with half of the mountain moving north and half moving south." Revelation 10:2, NIV, "He was holding a little scroll, which lay open in His hand. He planted His right foot on the sea and His left foot on the land." With this knowledge, which we should have as believers, is it prudent for us to keep filling our children's heads with false teachings? God's principles and values should be planted in their hearts. I would ask the true believers to flee from false gods!

AI, (artificial intelligence)

We also must be very careful not to ignore AI, (artificial intelligence), which is rapidly becoming a great tool of Satan. The potentials for evil are unlimited!

Fasting

My friends, we as true believers in our Lord and Savior, Jesus Christ, need to be very sensitive to God if He is asking us to fast. As we know, He always asks us to pray, especially when it comes to our leadership. President Trump needs our prayers, not just for salvation, but also for wisdom and knowledge in guiding our nation. Believers who are not phony always come together over the principles and values of their Lord and Savior. They do not back- bite and argue amongst themselves over the Word of God. I tell you the truth, as long as we, a nation, and the phony Christians continue to overlook and bow down to other gods through political correctness, entitlement, and equality, God's wrath will continue to fall. As a nation, we just get worse as times goes by. I ask you to do your homework and research on Moloch, Baal, and how we are to this day influenced by these gods in our church and nation. I write this as a warning. I hope we will all take it seriously. We should all stop our murmuring and do the applying of our risen King's Word!

Who is Moloch?

Moloch is the Biblical name relating to a Canaanite god associated with child sacrifice. The name of this deity is also sometimes spelled Molech, Milcom, or Malcam.

Who was Baal?

Baal was the name of the supreme god worshiped in ancient Canaan and Phoenicia. The practice of Baal worship infiltrated Jewish religious life during the time of Judges in the Bible. Baal was the god worshipped in many ancient Middle Eastern communities, especially among the Canaanites, who apparently considered him a fertility deity and one of the most important gods in the pantheon.

The Church must repent of Baal, Moloch, and other ancient gods and goddesses! The church just keeps silently serving them because it is tradition, and laziness, which promote compromise! Remember the Lord is coming back for a pure, cleansed bride! It is as plain as the nose on a clown's face that America is so confused they do not know what god they are serving. It has been my experience that most people do not know who Moloch is and yet most of America is serving Moloch. They have no understanding of Allah and who he is. Through the last few years of my ministry I have talked to those professing Christianity and say they attend church, but it astounds me how they know nothing about what the Word of God says regarding this subject. For instance God says, "I am the way and the truth and the life; no man comes unto Me, the Father, except through My Son Jesus Christ".

WARNING!

There are many among you who speak foolish things. For is it not true that I, the Father, have created all that you can see and not see? Have I not told you that I have placed the stars in the sky? And the moon and the sun to give you light? Yet you, who are foolish, choose to believe in other gods. You choose to chase after Baal and Moloch like you chase after the Easter rabbit. Am I not the one that has created your climate? I am the one who controls the wind and the seas. The one who calms the storms! Yet you who come to the temple whenever, whether inside or outside of the temple, and proclaim my name, you believe you do this? Is this your work, or my work? Is it not written that there will be those amongst you that will profess such dribble? And I will tell you "I knew you not"! And I will have you delivered out of my sight for eternity! Surely you must know only the wise know of one God, and that is through my son, Jesus Christ. I tell you the truth, the pathway to eternal life is through your Father's Word! Prophetic Word by Rev Mel Jolley

Challenge Leadership in the church

1 Chronicles 17:20, NKJV, "O Lord, there is none like you, nor is there any God besides You." Isaiah 44:6, NKJV, "I am the first and I am the last, and there is no God besides Me." It is obvious that history of the Christian church is not being taught and how can we learn from our history if we don't know the history? We need to ask questions and challenge our leadership in the church.

Chrislam

For those who are seeking the truth a warning for these serious times of deception! There are many faith based Universities that are actively destroying Christian principles by allowing staff members to seek and justify Chrislam. Therefore many denominational churches are embracing this false teaching. I can't think of any better reason for us to have a personal relationship with Christ and know God's Word ourselves. With so many Christians being deceived into so many false teachings such as New Age teaching, eastern doctrines, etc., the true believer needs to make their covenant with God and pray to clean out the cess pool of progressive, liberal, anti-Christ, untruths that are in the three branches of government.

Pagan Holidays

I have been thinking today about how hard it is to be Christ like and a "sold out Christian to the Lord". The fact is so many people who call themselves Christians and go to church on a regular basis, and who participate in Bible studies still want to cling to all of their "pagan holidays". They don't want to change anything for the Lord. At the same time they want to have a rating list of sins. One sin is greater than another. They say they understand mercy; however they do not understand that sin is simply that, sin. They don't want to accept God's way so they will justify serial killing of unborn children and euthanasia believing that it's not the same as being a "Ted Bundy, or green river serial killer". I know of an alcoholic who knows that he is an alcoholic, and says he is a Christian and has returned to drinking alcohol on a regular basis. What has happened to the scriptures where God says one must be born again and become a new creature in Christ? The sad thing is that even the spiritual leaders amongst us are being deceived in the same way by being "people pleasers" to the government and justifying other gods and their rituals. They don't celebrate the seasons and the days that the Lord has asked us to celebrate, instead they say this is past and not for today. I see no difference between these people and the people of the world. It's time to clean the sin out of the House of God. Don't measure the level of sin, because sin is sin whether one sin or a multitude of sin! Do not be supportive or co-dependent to those who choose to go the way of the world!

Two questions to ask progressives and liberals

1. Where does the Bible state that gender choice is of Christ?
2. Where does the Bible state that aborting unborn children is of Christ?

The liberals and progressives fight to legalize these sinful abominations and practices.

We must be wise in the ways of the Lord so that we be not deceived! There are many amongst us who do not understand the philosophy of Progressiveness, Liberalism, Socialism, Marxism, and Communism. The roots come from the evil one, Satan, when he came to Eve in the Garden of Eden and tempted her with the fruit of the tree of good and evil. Satan has deceived us as a nation to believe in "other gods". He has us believing that there are "other ways" in getting to heaven without going through Jesus Christ. Another example of his influence is the belief that if an unborn child is an "inconvenience", it can be disposed of. He is the one who authored "Ro verses wade" and "same sex marriage". Please read Job 1:6-12, in you Bible. This is how Satan does it. He seeks out those who are ignorant of God's Word, and preys on them by giving them a deviant mind. This especially applies to those who are in authoritative positions.

CHAPTER EIGHT
Inalienable Rights

Mel's Psalm

The Father says hush, hush now my child. It's time to be quiet and listen. I see you there trembling and afraid. I have always asked you to come out of the darkness and into the light where you can see the light. I know you hear the blood of the unwanted children crying out from the land and that of the people who have dared to love me and live by my principles and values. You will see that I am truly your Father, as you come closer to me and let me embrace you, until we become one. You will feel the serenity and peace as well as the love I have for you. I know you are hungering for something you can put your trust in. I've heard your heart say that you do not know who you can trust any longer. I want to take you out of that darkness and into the light where you no longer fight depression and anger. I know you feel a lot of bitterness with confusion, my child, but I am here, wanting to hold you on my lap and comfort you. You truly know I want to fill you with the Holy Spirit who will cause you to rejoice and dance. I want to hear utterances of praise and songs of music as sweet as honey coming from your lips all the while you are dancing my child. You know you have been given the gift of freedom of choice. I would not violate that gift. Do you hear me speaking to you my child? I have given many inalienable rights that are yours, that have come from only me.

Written by Rev. Mel Jolley

America's insanity

We are seeing an example of America's insanity. When it comes to the 2nd amendment, the right to bear arms, this shows you how the Leviathan spirit corrupts people's minds as well as blinding them to the truth of God's Word. Every American and Christian should know the first five rights of the Bill of Rights. Our rights are inalienable rights which means they come from God. This is a prime example of evil versus good. Evil wants to strip you of all your inalienable rights that God has given you. Evil does not want you to have a clear understanding of God's Word as well as the Bill of Rights and your Constitution. Whatever happened in Las Vegas and other mass killings, it isn't the weapon that actually does the deed, but it is the evil in the person that does the deed. When Cain slew Able with the jaw bone of an ass, he could have used any other object of choice. This shows the behavior of the Liberal and Socialist people of America, the ignorance that they have when it comes to God's Laws and values. A prime example of what happens to a nation when they take Christ out of the system.

Most state constitutions recognize all people have inalienable rights. We hold these truths to be self-evident, that **all men are created equal**, that they are endowed by their Creator with certain inalienable rights which among these are life, liberty and the pursuit of happiness.It is truly the anti-Christ spirit that is tearing out our foundation and Christian culture and lifestyle that God blessed the world and not just the United States through. As you notice these same deviate minded people are attacking a chapel in Oklahoma University to force the University to take out the cross from the chapel along with bibles and other Christian items. We the people stand by the Bill of Rights and our Constitution. We have the right of freedom of speech and this does not give anyone the privilege to disregard the God who gave you your inalienable rights.

CHAPTER NINE
Truth

Mel's Psalm 5

I find it hard to believe that you knew me before I was knitted in my mother's womb. But the truth lies in your Word. There are those who believe in predestination. However, your spoken Word tells us of your free will and this you would not break. In that I toil with choices. When I was a child, I did things as a child, as I learned of your word I did not know how to respond at first. But through suffering and tribulations and much pain I found that truth is your spoken Word not that of man. In the beginning was the Word and the Word was God. No longer have I the world to blame, or the prince of darkness, for now that I have experienced the truth and felt your Spirit in me, I have learned of accountability. It was your blood that was shed at Calvary. And that was sprinkled upon the mercy seat. So it is your mercy, not the mercy of man, and not what I do, but it is by what you did. This gives me the eternal life that I once sneered at and didn't understand. But you have made a way out of no way for all man. Yet I find myself grieving as much as one grieves for the passing of another into death not knowing if they have passed into eternal life. With your Spirit, which dwells within me, I know the truth I fear, not because I fear death, but because it is the separation of you from me.

Written by Rev. Mel Jolley

Truth is a choice, and one needs to accept it!

I can understand why there is a group of people who do not want to go or join a church. I was one of those. However, I needed to become a believer in the truth, who is Jesus Christ. Not a denomination, but to be true to my personal relationship with my Lord and Savior. We are to be different than those of the world. We are called to a higher standard.

For America to be redeemed, "We the people", who are called by His name, have to humble ourselves and pray for redemption. Redemption comes by the Word of God and the shed blood of Jesus Christ. Sometimes it may not feel good when the Holy Spirit convicts us of the changes we must make. Are we pliable and willing to change for the Glory of God and His righteousness and not that of man?

I feel God is revealing to me through this time period where so many prophecies are continuing to be fulfilled, all of these are signs of God speaking to His people. The believers in Christ know that these things will continue on and will even get worse until the people come to realize that He is Lord. Just the hurricane experiences in shutting down the refineries, the impact that will have on the market and economy will be astronomical! All these things point to the sin of our nation in condoning sins, in legalizing them or ignoring them. For those who don't know what this means this doesn't say much for them other than they don't seek the truth or have the desire to read God's Word to find out what it does mean. My heart grieves for all of those people who "unfriend God" because of the truth being spoken, thinking they can ignore it and it will go away. However the truth is not to be ignored and it "never goes away!" God doesn't need to change and will not change as His Word says. The responsibility is up to "We the people". You need to have the <u>willingness to accept the truth and make the change.</u>

Perhaps you are trying to identify the truth. Maybe you have been hunting for it, or wanting to know it's meaning, or its value, or even if it is tangible. I had been on this journey for many years until I found it, and it became real to me. **John 1:1, (KJV),** "In the beginning was the Word, and the Word was with God, and the Word was God." This identifies the truth that it is something tangible and that everyone can seek the truth any time during their lives.

Read in your Bible, Matthew 4:8-11

The devil took Jesus to a high mountain and showed Him all the glory of the kingdoms in the world. The devil told Jesus that he would give Him all this if He would fall down and worship him. "Be gone Satan! It is written, you shall worship the Lord your God and Him only shall you serve". Then the devil left Him, and the Angels came and ministered to Jesus. Even Jesus, the son of God was tested to see who he would follow! This scripture is good to remember when you are being tempted or tested in your faith.

"I am the way, and the truth, and the life"

John 14:6, (NASB), "⁶ Jesus said to him, "I am the way, and the truth, and the life; no one comes to the Father but through me." As we see this, we come to realize that there is a total opposite that pulls us away toward Satan, the author of lies. When we come to the point in life when we can accept God's Word to be the one which is the absolute truth, there will be peace and serenity in one's life. That is why we must seek truth in all things. Without the truth you have the decay of principles and moral values.

There is another passage that says in Romans 3:4, (NASB), "May it never be! Rather, let God be found true, though every man be found a liar, as it is written THAT YOU MAY BE JUSTIFIED IN YOUR WORDS, AND PREVAIL WHEN YOU ARE JUDGED." It would be prudent for us to take all things to God's Word to see if it is true or not. Otherwise it is easy for us to be deceived by the evil one.

Romans 3:4, (NKJV), "⁴ certainly not! Indeed, let God be true but every man a liar. As it is written: That you may be justified in your words, and may overcome when you are judged."

We are battling evil!

Some of you might find this shocking. We are not fighting a battle with politicians; the truth is we are fighting a battle against evil. People like Margaret Sanger, Madeline O'Hare, George Soros and others who have depraved minds. The only solution to our problems in the world and America is "we the people" change ourselves and come to the realization that all mankind is a "liar". There is only one truth. The truth is that we need to come to God and follow His principles and values. This includes all denominations, all people, all faiths, if each one of us do this, it is my belief that it would take only 10-15 percent of us to change the world. Wouldn't this inspire you to come to Jesus and listen to His words and not that of man?

All one can do is offer the truth. I hope I have been doing this by giving you books and documentaries to read and watch; and telling you to compare them to the Word of God. I know there will always be those who will deny science and history and will not make the time to study and find the truth to improve their life and the lives of others. By doing this, it affects where you live and the nation.

Masks

This time of year, thinking of Halloween, we think of pumpkins, masks, goblins and candy. There has come a time perhaps in our lives when we would want to seek the truth and take the mask and costumes off, no longer hiding who we really are. This takes overcoming fear and building trust, which only comes through knowing what is truth. As we seek the truth we can build trust in ourselves and others. This begins within us. Some of us may find ourselves wearing a "slug" costume.

Some scriptures from the Bible in the book of Proverbs reference the sluggard in various situations such as: Proverbs 6:9 (NIV), "How long will you lie there, you sluggard? When will you get up from your sleep?" (This makes you aware of your laziness). This makes us uncomfortable in our costume and aware of criticism as we leave the trail of slime. Proverbs 10:26 (NIV), "As vinegar to the teeth and smoke to the eyes, so are sluggards to those who send them." Read Proverbs 13:4 in your Bible. A sluggard is never satisfied because they covet more and more. They don't work hard for the goal; they do not focus on the process which is satisfying to the soul. They don't care about how they get the goal accomplished. Read these Proverbs in your Bible referring to sluggards. Once again because of their lack of hard work towards the goal, they don't take time to cultivate the goal so it is not accomplished! A sluggard believes he knows more than anyone else, including God!

Read these Proverbs in you Bible. Proverbs 20:4; Proverbs 23:19; and Proverbs 26:16. This is the time when the costume is taken off and we are tired of our old ways and want to become a good character with honesty and values. We want to be what God wants us to be, a person with principles and morals.

Read Proverb 30:24 and Proverb 30:25 in your Bible. We see this in ourselves. Let's unveil ourselves through the atonement of Jesus Christ. We can take that costume off and be what Jesus wants us to be.

Al Gore

For the entire Al Gore climate control cronies: When will you learn that God's Word is the truth? Anything else is but a lie! Genesis 8:22 (NIV), "As long as the earth endures, seedtime and harvest, cold and heat, summer and winter, day and night will never cease."

Attacking?

A lot of people are appalled at the truth of God. As a child of God I have the liberty and freedom to make judgement on what is righteous or non-righteous. If you spent time studying God's word, the Holy Bible, and His principles, you would be a better person and citizen. I don't see this as attacking anyone, it is the truth, if the truth convicts you, then that means you need to change. You need to read the Bible and read all the attacking things Jesus said, <u>if this is attacking!</u>

Don't be discouraged by the news and current events that you hear. There is hope. Hope is found in the truth. It would be nice if we could understand that the truth only comes from the Word of God. There are many phonies in this world who claim to know the truth. However the truth starts with each one of us individually. We must no longer compromise the truth. This is how we have lost the nation that we once knew and the Constitution we once lived by. It seems to me that it would behoove us to aggressively put a stop to compromising our principles and values. We have really shot ourselves in the foot by continually voting in and electing progressives and liberals and those who do not stand for the litmus test which is the truth. It only comes from the Word of God. Truth does not come from man.

Chapter Ten
Education for the Church

When will God's Children learn to "occupy" until He comes back? Luke 19:13,(KJV), "And he called his ten servants, and delivered them ten minas, and said unto them, "put this money to work, and occupy till I come."

Occupy

Military meaning of occupy could mean control by force. America's leadership from Commander in Chief and through the pentagon as well as a great number of our spiritual leaders have lost the vision that God has given us through His principles and values, as well as in our national documents such as the Constitution, Bill of Rights, Declaration of Independence etc. They are not applying what God meant when He said Occupy till I come. We have had some great leaders in the past, both spiritual and military who kept our nation a sovereign nation under the one true God in liberty and freedom for all. If we do not learn how to occupy by picking up the sword of Christ and become involved politically, from your local school boards all the way to the White House, our children will never see that bright shining city on the hill, or that true blaze of glory and freedom. I am saying this because we do have some people out there who are showing great leadership. They need our support, sweat, blood and labor. The 9/12 groups, Black Robe Regiment, Freedom Works, Mark Meckler, Convention of States.com, Ted Cruz, John Hagee, Franklin Graham, Elvira King, Glenn Beck, Mark Levin to name a few. There are many others.

Senior Care Facilities

Many have asked about ministering in care facilities. I happen to be of the opinion that "these lives matter". "All lives matter!" Perhaps this is the most crucial time of all, for some of them may not be leaving the facility unless they are passing on to eternal life. Maybe this is the last opportunity for a pivoting point in their lives, for forgiveness and the opportunity to do something good for others that the Lord would want them to do. Each one of them can have that opportunity to bring light and peace into someone else's life and affect the lives around them. Regardless of whether they are in a care facility or not, it's even those who are snowed by drugs or perhaps in a coma, traumatized, or a stroke victim, etc. It is still possible for them to have a change of heart and be a "doer" of God's Word at some level. I can't help but think about the quote "Jesus came to set the captives free". They are free indeed! So many of us are willing to "enable" others right into hell and forget about those who are sitting on the threshold of eternity. There are some good books out there that many of us can learn from. Joanie Erickson's biography and Gabe Murfitt's book, "My Message is C.L.E.A.R. for examples. Check out your Christian book store for others as well. Even while one is captive they can still think and pray in their minds. They can still hear the Word of God even though they may be "unconscious". The Spirit of the Lord crosses all boundaries. "Nothing can separate us from the love of God". We need to ponder these things much more often than we do because "these lives matter".

Christmas

Christmas in America is not about pagan gods. It's about the birth of the Christ child, who is the Son of God. I find it quite interesting that Bethlehem is sometimes called the city of David. Bethlehem is known as the "house of bread"! In Hebrew Beth-lehem is two words and means "house" (Beth as in Beth-el, "house of God") and "bread" (lehem). The Hebrew language is read from right to left. Bethlehem is the house of bread. Christ is the living bread. We all need to be nourished not only by natural bread, but "by every word that comes forth from the mouth of God" found in Deuteronomy 8:3 in your Bible. Read Acts 2:42, where the early church devoted themselves to the apostles' teaching and fellowship with breaking of bread and prayer.

We know Christ Jesus as the" Good Shepard", who provides His flock with food, "the bread of life". Now this brings us to the manger where Jesus was born. I looked at the definition of manger and this is what I found: A **manger**, or **trough**, is a structure used to hold food to feed animals. The word **manger** originally referred to **a feed-trough.**

Perhaps you have wondered about the star of Bethlehem, or the Christmas star that lit up in the sky over Bethlehem or the City of David and led the three wise men to see the Christ child. The Star of Bethlehem, also called the Christmas Star, revealed the birth of Jesus to the Biblical Magi, and later led them to Bethlehem, according to Christian tradition. The star appears in the nativity story of the Gospel of Matthew, where astrologers from the east are inspired by the star to travel to Jerusalem. There they meet King Herod of Judea, and ask where the king of the Jews had been born. Herod, following a verse from the Book of Micah interpreted as a prophecy, directs them to Bethlehem, to the south of Jerusalem. The star leads them to Jesus' home in the town, where they worship Him and give Him gifts. The wise men are then given a divine warning not to return to Herod so they return home by a different route.

Refrain from false gods

Americans should refrain from false gods and their teachings and stick to the God of the Bible. Read in your Bible, Galatians 1:8-9, where Paul said twice, that those who pervert the gospel would be cursed.

Many, who are responsible for the changes in the various Bibles available today, did not believe that Jesus was God and even a few did not believe in God at all. Knowing this, we can see why they were quite willing to change the Word of God. They leave out dozens of references to the deity of Jesus Christ, and they add words which tend to question His virgin birth and His substitutionary death (which fully satisfies atonement). Due to all the errors, omissions, and subtle changes in Bibles since 1881, Bible Probe highly recommends Christians use ONLY the Protestants original Authorized King James (1611).

Replacement Theology

I would like to talk about Christians or "wanna be Christians" which pertains to "most" denominations in the church. "Replacement theology" which includes one's principles and values is why it is extremely important for us as Individuals to be alert and studios about our walk with Christ. This is the belief that God rejected the Jewish people because of their rejection of Christ as the Messiah. It is believed that the Christians became the "favored or chosen" people and replaced the "apple of God's eye", the Jewish peoples. Hitler was one who believed this and actually thought he was doing God a favor by exterminating the Jewish people. Many Christians still believe this garbage and in their arrogance they send the Jews to hell with no concern for their souls or even a prayer! This is nothing but a tool of Satan because he hates the Jews because Jesus Christ is a Jew. Without the Jews rejecting Christ, the rest of humanity would not have salvation! Because their eyes were blinded, Jesus was crucified by capital punishment, the cross, and thus all peoples were granted salvation. That is why the scriptures say, "Salvation is from the Jews!" It also says that the Lord is the same today, yesterday and forever! Remember, we can't place the blame of our lost salvation on any one but ourselves because after all, we are the ones who are in charge of our salvation and destiny. You can look replacement theology up by googling it. It is no wonder many are suffering from depression and feeling of floundering and loss!

Bondservant

Question: "What is a bondservant?" **Answer:** A bondservant is a slave. In some Bibles the word *bondservant* is the translation of the Greek word *doulos*, which means "one who is subservient to, and entirely at the disposal of, his master". Other translations use the word *slave* or *servant*. This shows that we cannot serve two masters. Islam is diabolically opposed to God's salvation plan. The God of Abraham, Isaac and Jacob is a God of loving and restoring. The apostle Paul referred to himself as a bond servant of Jesus Christ. "I Paul, a bondservant of Jesus Christ, called *to be* an apostle, separated to the gospel of God", Romans 1:1, (NKJV).

Apostle Paul

When we study the life of the apostle Paul who experienced tyranny in his life, as well as persecution by man, it shows that whosoever chooses to follow after Christ shall and would expect to face persecution and most likely tyranny in their life as well. As we see in our own nation, America, tyranny is winning for now. Those of us who choose to follow after Christ should expect persecution and suffering as we see the falling away of the church while God is preparing the bride. The older we get we must be steadfast in our knowledge of God's Word and wisdom because we'll need to rely on the Spirit of God to show us the truth of

His fruit. Do not buy into deception for convenience sake or just because it sounds good and that it may give instant gratification. As we grow older, chronologically our minds can grow weak which allows Satan or his demons to rob us of our serenity and peace. This is why it is necessary to have good basic Christian principles and moral values. Be steadfast in them as you grow older. This is established growth in maturity.

Chapter Eleven

12 Steps and Twelve Promises

How many have heard that life is but a journey? When one is thinking of this they are most likely planning on seeing it as a trip. Since I am totally blind this entails a lot of planning. What am I going to use for transportation? How will I map this out in my mind? What signs must I look for? What is my final destination? I have come to realize that a lot of us do not give these things the importance of thought that they deserve. This causes us to go out of our way or stumble and fall, arguing, "I told you to go straight, instead of going the other way!" If life is a journey, what is your mode of transportation in your life? What will get you there? What is your map? What is your destination?

A confused mind

A person can have a confused mind. Yet he can ask the Lord for clarity, wisdom and knowledge. This person is showing he is willing to make changes in his life. Having the willingness to implement the Word of God, and conforming to God's principles and values, not conforming to the flesh;

he is willing to seek salvation through Jesus Christ. We are living in a season where the Lord has spoken that He will allow the people to be given over to a reprobate and depraved mind. This is their choice, and then there is little to no hope for salvation because of the unwillingness to change and conform to that of the Lord. They have given themselves over to the evil one. Read Romans 1 for an example. This is not hate speech, this is love speaking.

Reprobate

America needs to learn a new word, "reprobate". While we take an inventory of ourselves we don't hear enough of this from the pulpit. The only way we are going to save ourselves and our family members is through educating ourselves with God's Word. As we look at the word, "reprobate", it will be easy to tell where your political and spiritual leaders stand with regard to the use of this word.

Meaning of reprobate: noun1. A depraved, unprincipled, or wicked person: a drunken reprobate.2. A person rejected by God and beyond hope of salvation. Adjective 3. Morally depraved; unprincipled; bad. 4. rejected by God and beyond hope of salvation. Verb (used with object), reprobated, reprobating. 5. To disapprove, condemn, or censure. 6. (Of God) to reject (a person), as for sin; exclude from the number of the elect or from salvation.

Meaning of depraved: adjective: morally corrupt; perverted.

(Definitions are taken from The Free Dictionary by Farlex, found online.)

Refer to the meaning of reprobate above. A reprobate was used to describe, especially in Calvinism, a sinner who is not of the "elect" and is predestined to damnation. They were considered beyond hope of salvation and rejected by God. There's no way around it, a reprobate is a bad egg; the black sheep of the family, missing a moral compass. Other words used to describe them are deviant, evildoer, or a scoundrel. Selfish, depraved, disreputable, a reprobate is not known for his inner goodness. He is a reject of God! You can see how there are those who call themselves Christians "but they are not" because they are given over to this mind set. That is why it is so important that we take our moral inventory daily.

Read Romans 1:28-30. They didn't think it worthwhile to retain the knowledge of God, so God delivered them over to a depraved mind so they do what is not to be done. They were filled with all wickedness, evil, greed and depravity. They are full of envy, murder, strife, deceit and malice. They gossip, slander, hate God, are insolent, arrogant and boastful, they invent ways of doing evil; and disobey their parents.

When the Progressive Party started, their intent was to weaken the Word of God by taking these 12 steps out of the church and to stop teaching them from the pulpit. By replacing it with a Marxist idea of entitlement, a frame of mind which opposes the Declaration of Independence and the Constitution, it opposes the principles and values of God. Is there any church out there that teaches how to stand, apply, and be accountable? What are the consequences we are facing because we did not?

The Twelve Steps

These are taken from the 12 Steps for Christians, published by RPI Publishing.

1. We admitted we were powerless over our problem—that our lives had become unmanageable. (Romans 7:18-23)
2. Came to believe that God, through his son Jesus Christ, could restore us to sanity. (Romans 7:24-8:2, 1Corinthians 10:12)
3. Made a decision to turn our will and our lives over to the care of GOD. (John 1:12)
4. Made a searching and fearless moral inventory of ourselves. (James 1:21-25, Psalm 139:23-24)
5. Admitted to God, to ourselves, and to another human being the exact nature of our wrongs. (1John 1:9, James 5:16)
6. Were entirely ready to have God remove all these defects of character. (James 4:7-10)
7. Humbly ask him to remove our shortcomings. (1 John 1:9, Hebrew 4:14-5:3)
8. Made a list of all we had harmed, and became willing to make amends to them all. (Luke 19:8-10)
9. Made direct amends to such people wherever possible, except when to do so would injure them or others. (Matthew 5:23-24)
10. Continue to take personal inventory and when we were wrong promptly admitted it. (Psalm 32:1-7, Philippians 2:12-13)

11. Sought through prayer and meditation to improve our conscious contact with GOD, praying only for knowledge of His will for us, and the power to carry it out. (Philippians 4:5-9, 3:10-14)

12. Having had a spiritual awakening as a result of these steps, we tried to carry this message to others, and to practice these principles in all of life. (Philippians 2:3-5, Matthew 28:19-20)

Read these following passages: John 17:14, (NIV),"I have given them your word and the world has hated them, for they are not of the world any more than I am of the world." John 17:16, (NIV),"They are not of the world, even as I am not of the world." In reading these passages what does this say about our individual lives? Can we tell the difference between God's people and those who are just "church goers" who are living like people of the world? Do these scriptures cause us to take our own morale inventory? Is God calling us to a higher standard? Are we being asked to change our principles and values?

My prayer is for enough righteous people to pray that those among us would have the willingness as well as the desire to make changes in their personal life to become more righteous. This does not mean "holier than thou", but to truly change our ways and, about behavior pleasing to Christ. I would hope we would not vote for an unrighteous candidate at any time for the sake of compromising. We do not compromise our principles and values! Jesus did not compromise His principles and values! Always put Christ and the Kingdom of God first in all things.

Legalization of marijuana

Since the legalization of marijuana in 2012 there has been an increase in usage for medical as well as recreational. There are many different kinds of legalized recreational drugs. Marijuana will enhance any and all of them. This is why we as Christians must be aware that the legalization of recreational drugs is a direct open gate for Satan to enter into our minds. Those who have experienced drug usage know what I am saying is true. One drug will enhance another drug. Drug users will use this to perpetuate a longer state of euphoria or high. These drugs will compromise our thinking pattern and capability of making common sense decisions. In the beginning of the usage, there is a voice in yourself that is telling you that it has not made a difference in your life style and relationships. Over a period of time, however, people around you will see how it has affected your life style and relationships, as well as your attitudes. This can cause mild to deep depression. Legalized drugs can be alcohol, tobacco, vaporing, prescription drug abuse etc.

You have heard, "being true to thine own self is great wisdom". Very few understand this saying. **Romans 8:13, NIV,** "For if you live according to the flesh, you will die; but if by the Spirit you put to death the misdeeds of the body, you will live." **Luke 9:23, NKJV,** "²³ Then He said to them all, 'If anyone desires to come after Me, let him deny himself, and take up his cross daily, and follow Me". I believe one of the hardest lessons for us humans to learn is when we take our own inventory we need to be honest about it. What makes this difficult is our worldly flesh. Because God said "I am the truth and the way" our flesh does not want to accept it. Therefore it is our sinful nature to hesitate and in that hesitation we become deceived and that is where we are misled by Satan. For an example, this is where we lose it when we go to vote on legislations. This is why we need to take God's Word where ever we go and whatever we do.

Codependency

Codependency is a type of dysfunctional helping relationship where one person supports or enables another person's drug addiction, alcoholism, gambling addiction, poor mental health, immaturity, irresponsibility, or under-achievement. Among the core characteristics of codependency, the most common theme is an excessive reliance on other people for approval and a sense of identity.

There are many of us who come in the name of the Lord and do not understand true forgiveness or even the true meaning of mercy. Neither one of these pertains to or has anything to do with co-dependency. Co-dependency in its self is enabling sin. Quite often we confuse that. All of us have character defects or we inherit character defects. While we grow in the Lord we come to realize that sin is sin. It's our human nature that wants to allocate value to certain sins above other sins. This is why when we have forgiveness we need to allow each other to grow in the Lord. On a rare occasion someone may pray about a sin and God will deliver them from that sin which is a miracle in itself. However in most cases it takes practice, trials and tribulation to grow away from our sin nature. This is how we learn to trust in God and have faith in Him. That's why one can say, the goodness in me is the goodness from God and not of myself.

We are a better person and more Christ- like if we apply this in all things that we do.

Truth

I really feel a need to speak out on this subject again. It pertains to so many people who I love and have known as well as it may touch those that surround you. There are many who feel hopeless and alone, "an island"; probably even feeling overwhelmed, perhaps being stressed out to the max and looking for a great escape. Seriously I can relate to those people. When you have no hope because you don't believe in the truth or don't even know what to call the truth, which is the "Word of God", you can't have any faith. When there are no principles and values that are founded on the truth you can't have any serenity or peace in your life. This is why it is so important for us to release ourselves from church and denominations because of the corruption, and we must ground ourselves in the Word of God. Right now I believe the two most important books in the Bible concerning this matter are Proverbs, where we find our principles, values, as well as lifestyle. Then we have the Book of Job which teaches us how to survive persecution and mental anguish. I encourage you all to link yourselves with likeminded believers in God and focus on life style changing. With that comes an inner healing of emotions and mind. The dark cloud will soon be driven away, and the son will brighten your life with peace and serenity.

The Twelve Promises

(These are taken from the 12 Steps for Christians, published by RPI Publishing).

1. We are going to know a new freedom and a new happiness.
2. We will not regret the past nor wish to shut the door on it.
3. We will know peace.
4. We will comprehend the word "serenity."
5. No matter how far down the scale we have gone, we will see how our experience can benefit others.
6. That feeling of uselessness and self-pity will disappear.
7. We will lose interest in selfish things and gain interest in our fellow man.
8. Self-seeking will slip away.
9. Our whole attitude and outlook on life will change.
10. Fear of people and of economic insecurity will disappear.
11. We will intuitively know how to handle situations which used to baffle us.
12. We will suddenly realize that a power greater than us is doing for us what we could not do for ourselves.

When do these promises become real to us? At which time we realize that these promises are not just for alcoholics and drug addicts, but are meant for everyone when we allow the spirit of God to take control instead of our flesh.

Have you asked yourself how to be what you want to

become? That is the pivoting point of time that we start "new growth". One must ask themselves what is their rock of foundation to build upon? All of us have a purpose in our lives and find our directions from God. When we ask ourselves this question we have come to realize that there is something not quite right and we need to make a change of some kind. Another crucial word would be "character". All of us have character defects that God wants us to work on. These are defects that we will be working on until we go to be with the Lord. They are challenges in order to build our "Godly" character which will allow us to have the willingness to make changes in our lives. Let's say one wants to become a doctor. To become a doctor they must spend years in school studying, making high grades, and then many years of college and med school. After graduating from med school they are still practicing. Perhaps you have a surgeon who has been out of med school for quite some time. He or she specializes in a particular area. Yet they are practicing. So it is with us when we come to realize that there is something not quite right in our lives we need to go back to that true foundation and seek to find what isn't right in our lives and redirect our goal to that which is truly what we want to become.

Chapter Twelve
Presidential Election of 2016

Mel's Psalm 3

Oh Abba Father! How long must I exist with the stench of death that fills my nostrils? Your Spirit has slain me. I fall prostrate before thee. You have greatly given me many gifts. But yet when I walk into the House of Prayer, often I do not find you there. My eyes gaze upon benches with dusty bones and moths that flutter around me. How long must I persevere to see the spirit flow through? I must know that you are gathering your chosen people who follow after you. When must you call the bride of Christ home? When my flesh cries for the truth and I hear my brothers and sisters cry out to God. When wrong has become right and right has become wrong. You have warned me time and time again of wolves in sheep's clothing. And even those who call themselves theologians will be deceived. But yet I, who am blind, must persevere until I can see you with eyes that you would give me. Blessed Father, come as the Messiah. I long for thee. So be it.

Written by Melvin Jolley

People of faith

People of faith in God know that God will never force Himself on anyone. It's the same in elections. He allows the people to choose the direction they wish to go. I think one would choose the most Christ- like person, going by the lifestyle that they have displayed to us. We can measure it with what the Word of God says about lifestyles. God's plans will never be changed because of man; however man can slow the process through repentance and change of lifestyle. You must understand that God doesn't need the change, but rather, we the people, need to change. For we who are steadfast in Christ, find it pathetically humorous in what some of us are willing to settle for.

Presidential election of 2016

In our presidential election of 2016 we had the opportunity to vote for a person of Integrity, principles and morale standards. It was the first time in a long time that we had more than one choice that met these qualifications.

A friend of mine asked me about Donald Trump. He was quite impressed with him. My reply to him was "he is saying what you want to hear now, however, his record and behavior of the past speaks for itself. It's obvious that the man, Donald Trump, does not have the same principles that our forefathers of this nation and God have". We the people have to uphold these standards and bring them back. This goes for any political office and race. We need to be sure that we do our research. Don't just take someone else's word.

There are many wolves with sheep's' clothing. We need to be aware of them.

We the people need to demand more from the church than what we are getting from the pulpit. If we don't, we need to change the situation, or find a place where we will be fed and taught how to uphold these biblical principles. I am tired of my nation being run by serial murderers, homosexuals, gun runners, drug addicts, liars, and those who choose to believe that treason is ok. We do not need new laws and haven't for years. We just haven't been upholding the laws we have and our constitution. Do you think it's time to give God a chance?

Democratic debate-Caliphate in U.S.A.

In listening to the democratic debate I want to bring to our attention that not one of the candidates spoke out on behalf of liberty or the Constitution. Neither did they have anything to say about Jesus Christ. It was obvious that every one of them were communist, socialist with the mind of "one -world order." Not one of them spoke a word of truth but was very blatantly deceitful in spinning tales of lies. They were so blatant it reminded me of a spoof on Saturday Night Live! However, I want to take this time to say what is going on in the majority of the churches in our area is no different. The churches are going by "their agenda," rather than God's. Our board of directors and pastors are not giving us instruction on how to use information or tools. The churches leadership is not preparing us for what is coming. All I hear is "wait upon the Lord and pray." This allows Satan and the anti-Christ movement to come in, invade and take over. God will deliver us from evil. I tell you the truth right now, God will only deliver those who choose to act upon His word, principles and values with firm reliance and endurance. Those who choose to sit on their hands and be silent and not participate in their personal salvation, or their land, He will wash His hands clean of. The outer court people coming in the name of the Lord are blind to the urgency of the hour. They are not prepared. They are going without oil in their lamps and faking their way through darkness. What happened in Washington D.C. with the Million Man March? The title of Louis Farrakhan's speech was "In the name of Allah"; are we prepared for this kind of thinking? What about the launch of strong cities network? Are we so blinded that we don't see the caliphate happening in our own yard?

Candidates

We all know about Ahmed Mohamed, the "clock boy". President Obama had him come to the White House in order to honor his bad behavior in the name of Allah. It is obvious what his motives were and his behavior. Now we see our government leadership, media, and the school system honoring bad behavior instead of focusing on values and principles. This has been a prime example of the social cancer disease that we have to deal with. I say all of this to show that America truly has a two party system, that of Anti-Christ "evil" and that of righteousness which are "kingdom" principles and values. I believe that there was goodness to look forward to as far as presidential candidates for choices. We had good choices. Dr. Ben Carson was very impressive with the fire he has gone through and the wisdom and knowledge that he has. Talk about integrity, with principles and values, he had them all. He was rock solid on all issues, foreign and domestic. I was also very impressed with Bobby Jindal who is very outspoken and clear on all issues as well. Ted Cruz I liked from the very beginning. He is definitely a Constitutional man. These candidates were proven and tested as excellent candidates for the presidency.

I questioned the integrity of any one who calls themselves a Christian or spiritual leader and yet they would support someone like Donald Trump. He boldly bragged about his vices and willingness to compromise his soul when it comes to things of the Lord. He saw no sin in himself.

It's easy for us to tell somebody else that they are in denial, while we sit in denial ourselves. These things were so prevalent to me while I was listening to CPAC. I observed the destruction of the Republican Party before my eyes! Where there is faith, there is hope. Some of you have heard me say that there are people who were appointed and anointed by God for times such as these. We have heard God speak of them in the scriptures. I truly believe that Ted Cruz was that man. This said, it doesn't diminish the faith of Ben Carson or any other believers who uphold the principles and standards of God. The division of the candidates went on too long. Would it not be prudent for us as believers to rally around the person who is appointed of God? It's was a clear sound choice I thought!

Ted Cruz

I believed that Ted Cruz was the man who was born for this time and was appointed and anointed by God to carry the torch of liberty and freedom as well as righteousness. He was the answer to our prayers for a righteous man with godly principles and he believes in the Constitution that was given to us by God Almighty to form this great nation. Where was your faith Christians? Do you actually pray and not believe that your prayers will be answered? So many of you forsook Ted Cruz because you had no faith and you listened to the devil saying Cruz had no chance. Too many of you voted for a godless man because you didn't have faith in the one that God provided you with. Just as God said "I am the Lord thy God and I change not, I am the same yesterday, today, and forever." You still do not believe and your unbelief will give you what you deserve.

I want to encourage you to see the movie, "Pilgrims Progress". Perhaps then you will realize that this campaign was about fighting to get America out of the cess pool of evil. It is a journey about every one of us in our walk with the Lord and the process of salvation.

Moral Inventory

A Question for us, do we understand what the word boundary means? How do we identify with it? Myself, my boundaries are founded in the **B**asic **I**nformation **B**efore **L**eaving **E**arth (Bible) manual. It seems quite clear to me that Ted Cruz is a person who understands boundaries. He knows how to uphold them for the best interest of not just his family but our nation as well. This goes without saying he also has a clear vision on principles and values and how to uphold these things. His vision is not a new vision but it's a vision of restoring the truth which is God's Word without labeling it with some man made denominational sticker or "label". Each of us needs to interject this same standard and philosophy at our local level. By the way for those who didn't understand why things got so heated and frustrated around these candidates go to the Word of God and see that any time you take a stand the majority of the people are going to have distaste for these issues. They say they want them, but their actions oppose it because they really want greed, big government and the pleasures of sin.

Now is the time that we should focus on the Lord, in silence, in prayer and wait upon the Lord to see how many of us, we the people, have chosen to follow God's principles and values and not that of man. The season of tribulation is coming upon us. We need to be steadfast in our choices and in whom we choose to follow.

This is my opinion.

There is no quick fix for what is happening in the world situation. Honestly, I don't believe it will make much difference on whom our President actually is for the simple fact that we have gone too far as a nation in the direction of denying the one true God and His principles. It would have been nice to have a God fearing man as our next leader, such as Ted Cruz. He would have prolonged the fall of our nation, however man cannot change God's perfect plan. God has given us the choice. As an individual people we seek His kingdom that gives us the freedom of choice to be under His grace. There is no grace in our nation under the control of people who are anti- constitutionalists and not liberators of free man and choice, which can only come from Jesus Christ. This is what our nation was founded on and our Forefathers warned us that this would happen if we walk away from our principles and values. The handwriting was not just on the wall, it was in the Word of God and in the words of our founders who came to this nation.

About the convention

I was not surprised how disorganized everything was. I was glad to see those who protested by walking out of the convention, or just not showing up. I was glad to see the support that the people showed by this means and hoped to see more support because this was not the Republican Party that we knew. It is just another form of the Socialist-Democratic Party. I doubt if I will watch any more of this circus again. There is not a decent party to represent "We the People" and our nation any longer. I guess one would say I am mourning for what we are losing or already have lost, America! Please put your trust in God only. This is the time to turn to Jesus.

I think it's time for us to have mercy for each other. Allow yourself to vote your conscience and not expect others to vote your way. When a person votes their principles and values that is what they are doing. Allow them to do so and leave it at that. Some people vote Libertarian; write in a name, the Green Party, Hillary, Trump etc. We don't need to give peer pressure to those who prefer someone else other than Donald or Hillary, or whoever is running. What difference will it make in the long run anyway? Just remember only in America are you able to have such moral, fine upstanding candidates like these two to choose from! (I'm being sarcastic!)

My thoughts on the Presidential Candidates:

Many good hearted people who call themselves Christians voted for the man- child, Donald Trump. They should not feel bad about it. However, I feel they need to educate themselves on what this means. I'm not speaking politically but biblically as well. As far as Hillary Clinton goes I regretfully feel sorry for those who are in such deception. She needs our prayers for salvation and a change of heart. Pray for those who voted for her as well. Maybe someday the light will shine on what principles, values and morals truly are. I see no integrity what-so- ever! Without God there is no integrity.

By looking at the social media on the computer, a thought came to my mind, about just how much the people's thought processes have changed over the years. Especially those who claim to know the Lord. If we think back a year ago or so and during the primaries, at how many choices we had for Presidential candidates. There were at least four who had a good understanding of the Constitution. But we the people did not want them. Ted Cruz dropped out, and we were left with Trump and Hillary, two of the most dangerous vipers, which left us with <u>no</u> choices really. Evan McMullin who was running on the Independent ticket, became my choice. He is a man that has a good understanding of the Bible and principles and values with a clear understanding of the constitution. Are we the people, who are Christians, willing to stand for what is righteous and right? Are we willing to sacrifice whatever it takes to win this battle against evil and support the convention of states or do we turn our nation over to Donald Trump or Hillary? They are both liars. Help from the church was not there. Only God's remnant of people! If only Christians stood together and voted no for both Hillary and Trump, making a stand for righteousness! If only they had as much faith in God as they did for Trump who they believed would miraculously change and all of a sudden be a "savior" of America.

I watched the presidential debate and I thought Donald Trump was definitely the "winner". I don't approve of him or Hillary but I do think he made some important points in the debate and did very well.

I also watched the Governor's Debate for Washington State. I truly thought Bill Bryant won it hands down. I really liked his plans to improve our state, education and economy. While we are at it, it's time for Patty Murray to retire. Let's get some new blood that can make a difference. She is big business, big government, socialist, who will not keep a balanced budget.

For your eyes

Are your eyes open so that you can see the truth and what I have shown you? Is it not true that I created Adam from the dust; and his help mate, Eve, from the rib? Did I not breathe the breath of life into him? As I created him in my image, so did I to you! Did you not see where I said I knew you before you were created in your mother's womb? Where that seed of life started knitting you? I have a purpose for all mankind, even the one that was chosen for you to fulfill. Did I not warn you not to spill blood through killing on the land? For that innocent blood will cry out to me! Yet you see there in your darkness you turned away from me and sodemnized with your own kind when I gave you appropriation with your bride. Then still in the darkness of night the gift of life that I entrusted with you; you disposed of as trash! Even with your own eyes you have read the truth that there will be no uncleanness in my Kingdom. Yet I have prepared a place for those that have turned their backs against my will and failed to see the light of my glory.

Written by Rev. Mel Jolley

For your ears

You were asked to come into the garden to kneel and council with your Lord. You may cry tears of remorse through stress; you may sweat droplets of blood. Yet I will remain faithful. And knowingly, as I drink from my Savior's cup, I know that betrayal lies in the darkness and waits for me. As I go through this time of tribulation, my Lord promises me, as I remain holy with Him, I will have eternal life in heaven where His glory is the light from the fountain of the throne where the water gushes up. I don't just bathe my feet, but I am totally submerged in baptism with Him. For there is eternal life for all but I choose to spend it in my mansion that He has prepared for me.

Written by Rev Mel Jolley

We should ask ourselves, where did we go from here after the elections? Regardless of which candidate got into office, what did it do to change you and your life style or relationship with God? Have we come to the realization that America has completely changed from what it once was? Do we continue to work in restoring the constitution? Do we continue to restore God's principles and values, and the building of the foundation of our families and nation? Should we just throw our hands up and give up and allow the evil one to continue the destruction process? I'm asking this because I sense that people are thinking this is not as bad as it really is. They are not taking these questions seriously.

Chapter Thirteen
Man- Child

"Obomination"

Eight years ago I had a friend help me make a Video called "Obomination". I handed this video out to Christian friends and Pastors. It was created to expose Obama for whom or what he really is. I received a lot of criticism from "do gooder" Christians. They would say things like it was prophesized that Obama will receive Jesus Christ as his personal savior, that he would have a "Saul experience" and become a true man of God. Here we are in 2018, and I still see him as the son of perdition! His works will be carried on through the man-child (Trump). I do not believe that either one of these, Obama or Trump was appointed by God for anything except to fulfill prophecy, just like Judas, who betrayed Jesus. Man's sins, lust, and greed give Obama and Trump the power that they have. It certainly is not motivated by principles or values from God!

This is a very difficult topic for some unless you do your research and study. I want to make it clear that it was not my intention; I have never said that Obama is the Anti-Christ. But remember that his part in this is not finished!

So let it be known that I was talking about the man- child and the son of perdition. I believe in every generation there is an Anti-Christ figure, and son of perdition figure that is a possibility. Many will come in the Anti-Christ spirit. Only God knows what generation this will happen. There are many factors that are happening in the same time that will bring all of this about. If you have noticed, many nations are going bankrupt in their economies. The whole banking system of the world is on the verge of collapse. No one knows this better than George Soros. This puts in play the digital, cashless society. Many other factors are taking place. Islam and CARE are just as vital to bringing this about as Russia, the bear from the North, China and North Korea. All are participating. Turkey comes into play also because of the bear from the North. The American economy is very strategic in this because when it falls things really speed up! I know there is a lot here to think about and to study out of God's Word but if we don't understand what is coming our way in the world we are sluggards and fools! This is why all of us need to be doing our part in the smallest ways to make a stand for righteousness and be counted on the Lord's side.

Donald Trump, the man-child.

The Urban Dictionary defines a man- child as an adult male who still possesses psychological traits of a child such as whining, pettiness, passing blame for their own underdeveloped judgement, and not stepping up to the plate when they should. Secretly he finds 3rd grade bathroom humor amusing. He connects with his children as another child rather than a father. He has an overall insecurity in who he is, as a man. He is a bully insisting on his own way. He often marries a type "A" woman, who usually is first born or an only child in her own family. The man- child will attempt to mask his lack or compete with peers with material possessions. They have a need to impress their peers.

I believe that Obama set up, through Satan, a complete agenda for a man- child to come into play to fulfill scripture. If you listen to everything that Donald Trump has said in interviews and debates even including the sarcastic remarks he has made to women on various occasions and displaying his ignorance on overseas policies. Not being able to come up with a full agenda on how to solve problems. Could this be the man-child that the scripture talks about?

I am not sharing a conspiracy theory, however we must be aware that there are many Pharisees and naysayers who deny the truth even when they hear it, or see it happening before their eyes. I talked about the "Son of Perdition" in the past and the man-child. I covered this subject pretty well in detail. Most of us do not understand or take the time to learn about this subject. However, I want to share about a pamphlet booklet called, "Overthrow!", by Matthew Vadum. You can get it through David Horowitz, Freedom Center. This pamphlet focuses on Obama who is likened to the "Son of Perdition". I am not saying Obama is the "anti-Christ." However, the pamphlet gives us a small glimmer of insight on how he can be the "Son of Perdition." Even prior to him becoming President he was being groomed to totally destroy the United States and the western world. You can tell by his activities and the people he surrounded himself with including his wife, Michelle, in setting up his empire to destroy the Bill of Rights and the Constitution, while mocking Christianity, knowing that most Americans have a short attention span and are lazy thinkers and what parables call "sluggards". I would highly recommend reading this booklet and seeing just how evil Obama, as well as the Clintons are, and the part that Samantha Powers played while in office, to destroy us. Most people do not realize that Hillary, as well as Obama, committed treason while in office by sending a plane load of money to our enemies and also the Benghazi incident, with Hillary saying, "What difference does it make now?" Through this we can see how Trump is being used as the man- child trying to restore some dignity back to America. We will never see the land of the free and brave with freedom for a true American again because the shadow government has exploited the takeover of the true "America".

For those people who are believers and have some knowledge of scripture and have researched the "man -child" in Revelation, you have an advantage in understanding what made this particular voting time or election so biblically crucial. We see these explicit character defects of the man-child in Donald Trump. We should not be shocked or angry that he made it into office. It is a fulfillment of prophecy. However that does not mean that we should have voted for him. It's all the more reason to vote for God's principles and values. This was your time to stand for God and God's principles. The prophecy came to pass because God knows the people's hearts and that for the most part; they are wicked and vote for evil. We will all be judged by God, according to how we vote. If you choose evil, then you will answer to God about your choice. This is a barometer on where we are spiritually, as a nation.

I felt that something was witnessed to my heart. If I am to believe scripture, I see a direct correlation to Donald Trump being the man-child, Obama being the son of perdition, and that if the United States is the House of Israel, this would mean that Hillary Clinton could not be the president. Scripture will continue to be fulfilled because the church and leadership has not truly repented; and continues their wicked ways of not teaching the principles, values and boundaries of God. They are not willing to put on the full armor of God so therefore we will not just lose the Bill of Rights and our Constitution, but America will cease to be the America we have known. The remnant of God is preparing for Ezekiel 38 to come into play now. There has been a remnant of God's people who have been warning about this for over ten years. Our spiritual leaders have done nothing but turn a deaf ear and have ignored God's warnings.

There seems to be a lot of confusion on the son of perdition and the man- child. For those who are confused, my prayers go out to you. If you haven't studied the man-child in Revelation, I would recommend it. One has to do their homework and research along with the guidance of the Holy Spirit. The man-child does not necessarily have to be a Christian or a non-Christian. He will rule with an "armed fist". This is what is so appealing to Donald Trump fans. With this in mind, I want to make my comments to those who listened to Donald Trump's speeches while running for president. Did you pay attention to what he was saying about himself and the words he used? Examples: "I am the only one who can". "I will do it". "I will get it done". "I am a law and order presidential candidate". Did you listen to what the crowd was yelling, "yes you will, and yes you will"! Donald Trump is not God or the son of God. I heard Donald Trump's acceptance speech and my thought was that he did say what the people wanted to hear and what they needed to hear perhaps. This did not negate my belief that he could be the man- child. He delivered his speech beyond a doubt, as a man-child would.

After the democratic and republican conventions were over, it was time to ponder upon what the Word of God says concerning these two "Characters". You heard with your own ears what came out of their mouths. It was the time to deliberate and focus on God's Word and do what your conscience told you. It was nobody's place to tell anyone who to vote for or not to vote for. However the Word of God gave us the ultimate guide line to go by. That is why I spent so much time on Facebook sharing the materials and God's Word with you as I did. Speaking for myself, Obama is the son of perdition. I did my research on Obama, Donald Trump and Hillary Clinton. I believe Obama is the son of perdition, and Donald Trump is the man-child. It leaves me one place to go and vote for God's principles and values. That means that yes I have a full understanding of whom and what the man-child is and I could not give a vote to Hillary. I had to vote 3rd Party.

Donald Trump was not the choice that God would have us make. In saying this, neither was Hillary. We had the opportunity to choose a "Godly man" and we passed up the opportunity and we got what we deserved instead. We the people, who includes some of those who come in the name of the Lord, made this choice and we cannot blame God. Those who have assurance in Christ will find peace. Prophecy is being fulfilled through the choices of man whether "Godly" or not. I had principles and morals' that told me I could not vote for Hillary or Donald Trump.

After listening to Trump's message of Faith, I would like to say that it did sound good. However, I warned the people they just might get what they want. If it was truly Trump who they desired, I believe that God was very capable and willing to give him to them as their leader. I personally have not seen this man confess that he went before the throne of God, and asked God for forgiveness of his sins and guidance and direction for himself and our nation. I still hear a gong when he speaks and it's not a clear crystal bell sound. He speaks like a dictator and sounds like a spoiled child who is a bully and gets his way at any cost. I still hear impure thoughts and language with bitterness flowing from his lips. I can see the fulfillment of God's Word coming to pass through this man-child.

I got to the point where I hoped the people would get Donald Trump for president. It appalled me how many people claimed that they wanted a "Godly man" with integrity and principles. When the opportunity presented itself they denied it. (Ted Cruz) Why is it that they think that a "Godly man" with integrity and principles has to walk on water? But yet they clamor for a Donald Trump or are willing to go with Hillary Clinton? This tells me just how sick we are as a nation and no one understands integrity or principles. How can we stand for principles and values when we don't know what principles and values are? We can't have integrity when we consume and speak out lies? It is so true that America will fall as she continues to deny Christ for the simple reason that Americans have hope through God's Word, and yet they deny it instead of living by it!

Chapter Fourteen
God's Calendar

It's my hope that God's people will realize how important it is for us to go by His calendar and not that of a calendar based on just the sun or just the moon, known as the pagan calendar. As you will notice, most churches go by the pagan calendar. For more information about this as well as your Jewish heritage I would suggest you to read a book by Mark Blitz called "God's day planner". This is available through Amazon.com.

What do we know about Apostle Paul? We know that he was a magnificent man of God. In saying this we must understand that he had faults at the same time just as we all do. Did you know that he wrote almost half of the New Testament? One of the things I would like to bring up however that most of us don't realize, the Apostles started a disservice to us by encouraging the Christians to "throw the baby out with the bath water", so to speak, meaning their Jewish heritage which has crippled the church to this day. The Apostles never changed the Sabbath from Saturday to Sunday. They still observed the Sabbath on Saturday. The monies collected from the believers was done on Sunday to avoid the thievery taking place and the assembling together was safer on Sunday than on Saturday because of persecution going on. As far as the customs, and the laws and the holy days observed and the feasts celebrated, these were all thrown out. This is a very vital part of our Jewish heritage and is all about what Jesus saved us from besides our personal sins! Without the knowledge of this part, how can we truly understand what salvation is all about? So many things that Christ is, is in the laws, the customs, and the feasts and holy days observed. This is because it is linked to the fulfillment of prophecies. These are actually the days that we were given by God to observe. If you study these things you will see how each holy day and feast applies to Christ, which Jews have been observing blindly since the times of Moses. If you have noticed many of your New Testament churches give the impression that Paul is equal to God. However he was no different than any of us. Paul was very aware of this as you can see this battle in his writings, that he fought the battle of dying to the flesh. Many of us can learn through the example of his life if we would allow the Holy Spirit to witness Paul's life style and his behavior while we read his writings. Remember, Jesus Himself said that He came to fulfill the law, not to replace it! Just because we are no longer under the law, but grace, does not give us an excuse to not know the law, the customs, and celebrate the feasts and holy days that God ordained.

The Truth about the Sabbath

I hope this will cause you to give some thought about who changed the Sabbath from Saturday to Sunday? Or the 7th, to the 1st day of the week? Nowhere in the Bible do we find that Christ or the Apostles ordered that the Sabbath be changed from Saturday to Sunday. We have the commandment of God given to Moses to keep holy the Sabbath day that is the 7th day of the week, "Saturday".

Sunday was chosen by the authority of the one holy "Catholic Church." Constantine, the first Christian Roman emperor, was responsible for many of the Christian traditions formed and practiced today. Constantine was the first Roman emperor to convert to Christianity. He played an important role in the proclamation of the Edict of Milan in 313, A.D. which declared religious tolerance for Christianity in the Roman Empire. In 325, A.D., the Nicaea council produced the statement of Christian belief known as the 'Nicene Creed'. The Church of the Holy Sepulchre was built on his orders at the site of Jesus' tomb in Jerusalem and became the holiest place in Christendom. Constantine was responsible for The Papal claim to temporal power in the High Middle Ages. He is venerated as a saint by the Eastern Orthodox and Catholic Church. He has historically been referred to as the "First Christian Emperor," and he did heavily promote the Christian Church.

Constantine was the first emperor to stop Christian persecutions and to legalize Christianity along with all other religions and cults in the Roman Empire. Constantine was over 40 when he finally declared himself a Christian, writing to Christians to make clear that he believed he owed his successes to the protection of the Christian High God alone. Throughout his rule, Constantine supported the Church financially, built basilicas, and granted privileges to clergy such as exemption from certain taxes. He promoted Christians to high office, and returned property confiscated during the Diocletian persecution. His most famous building projects include the Church of the Holy Sepulchre, and Old Saint Peter's Basilica Bridge. He built the Arch of Constantine to celebrate his triumph. The arch is decorated with non-Christian images. Constantine did not patronize Christianity alone. After gaining victory in the Battle of the Milvian, the goddess Victoria, at the time of its dedication, he made sacrifices to gods including Apollo, Diana, and Hercules. Absent from the Arch are any depictions of Christian symbolism. Constantine legislated that the venerable Sunday should be a day of rest for all citizens; He also issued a decree banning Christians from participating in state sacrifices. After the pagan gods had disappeared from his coinage, Christian symbols appeared as Constantine's attributes.

The reign of Constantine

The reign of Constantine established a precedent for the position of the emperor as having great influence and ultimate regulatory authority within the religious discussions involving the early Christian councils of that time. Constantine himself disliked the risks to societal stability that religious disputes and controversies brought with them, preferring where possible to establish orthodoxy. His influence over the early Church councils was to enforce doctrine, root out heresy, and uphold ecclesiastical unity; what proper worship, doctrines and dogma consisted of was for the Church to determine, in the hands of the participating bishops. Constantine enforced the prohibition of the First Council of Nicaea against celebrating the Lord's Supper on the day before the Jewish Passover (14 Nisan). This marked a definite break of Christianity from the Judaic tradition. From then on the Roman Julian Calendar, a solar calendar, was given precedence over the lunisolar Hebrew Calendar among the Christian churches of the Roman Empire. Constantine one of the leading figures of the early Christian church left the door wide open to bring large numbers of people into the church by accepting pagan ways. This is one of the reasons why Christians do not celebrate the same holidays as the Jews or use the same calendar. The Leviathan Spirit was well at work!

Dr. Edward T. Hiscox, read a paper before a New York ministers' conference, Nov. 13, 1893, and it was reported in the " *New York Examiner*", Nov.16, 1893. This is what it said: *"There was and is a commandment to keep holy the Sabbath day, but that Sabbath day was not Sunday. It will be said, however, and with some show of triumph, that the Sabbath was transferred from the seventh to the first day of the week.... Where can the record of such a transaction be found? Not in the New Testament absolutely not.*

"To me it seems unaccountable that Jesus, during three years' intercourse with His disciples, often conversing with them upon the Sabbath question . . . never alluded to any transference of the day; also, that during forty days of His resurrection life, no such thing was intimated.

"Of course, I quite well know that Sunday did come into use in early Christian history . . . . But what a pity it comes branded with the mark of paganism, and christened with the

name of the sun god, adopted and sanctioned by the papal
apostasy, and bequeathed as a sacred legacy to Protestantism!"

God established the Sabbath day in the Old Testament.
Jesus the son of God recognized and kept the Sabbath
throughout the New Testament. Scripture reveals that the
Messiah will continue the Sabbath. It seems to me that a
lot of us Christians need to continue to study the Word
of God and realize how much Satan has robbed us of our
Godly heritage. For years I have been slammed by my own
Christian brothers and sisters because I have always obtained
and recognized the true Sabbath for what it is. Once again
we must become new creatures in Christ in following His
word, the truth, and not that of man.

More on the Sabbath

Scripturally I believe the truth being that God created
the heavens and the earth in seven days. We as Christians
need to realize that He is a God of order. Point being, that
He rested on the seventh day. It is my feeling that there are
many of us who come in God's name, who do not rest on
the seventh day of a given week. We don't focus on body,
soul, and mind to rejuvenate ourselves spiritually, or refresh
ourselves which completes our purpose and relationship with
Him. Many of us totally deny a Sabbath day of honoring
God, and giving ourselves to Him in worship; forsaking the
things of the world. We all do ourselves injustice when we
do not honor the 4th commandment.

CHAPTER FIFTEEN
House of Judah and House of Israel

To understand what is happening in the world as well as America, we must look at the two houses in the Bible. Let's take a look at Jacobs twelve sons' (the twelve tribes of Israel).

Reuben, Simeon, Levi, Judah, Issachar, and Zebulun were birthed by Leah.
Dan and Naphtali were birthed by Bilhah.
Gad and Asher were birthed by Zilphah.
Joseph and Benjamin were birthed by Rachel.

Reuben is the first born and with the first born comes all the blessings; however Reuben did something to lose that blessing. He slept with his father's wife, Bilhah. You will find this in Genesis 35:22 and in Genesis 49:4. We will also find out when we start talking about America and Ezekiel 38, that Reuben is a descendent from Gog which becomes a player in the last days with America.

Levi becomes the ministering tribe and actually does not take on tribal land and we will find out later that someone else gets to be part of the 12 tribes because of this.

Jesus comes from Judah, but Judah ends up taking on the name Jew and ends up becoming the Jewish state of Israel. Judah carry's on the blood line of Jesus. Judah will also be part of the house of Judah.

Joseph ends up having two boys, Ephraim and Manasseh. These two boys will get adopted by Jacob and the blessing that we were talking about earlier with Reuben; Ephraim gets that blessing which ends up becoming the 13th tribe of Israel and becomes a huge part in Bible prophecy.

Now you have to understand that these groups (12 tribes) are not yet "Jews" and Moses and Jacob were not "Jews" yet. At this point in the Bible there are no "Jews" yet; we will get to this in 1kings 10 and 16. So when you also read about the 12 tribes of Israel in Revelation which is not a Jewish passage, this will all make better sense when we get to splitting of the tribes. The 12 tribes did their thing as they got closer to the splitting, they listened to God, and they did not listen to God, they had a couple of people who ruled over them that were corrupt. The 12 tribes of Israel is very important to understand because remember that the prophets, Jesus, the disciples and in Revelation they are on a new heaven, new earth, and the 12 tribes are VERY important to understand.

THE SPLITTING OF THE 12 TRIBES OF ISRAEL HOUSE OF JUDAH

It all starts in 1 Kings 11, and in 11:31-32 NKJV. It says, "And He said to Jeroboam, Take for yourself ten pieces, for thus says the Lord, the God of Israel: "Behold, I will tear the kingdom out of the hand of Solomon and will give ten tribes to you." V.32, "But he shall have one tribe for the sake of my servant David, and for the sake of Jerusalem, the city which I have chosen out of all the tribes of Israel."

So now you have two tribes, ten become the house of Israel and two become the house of Judah. With Judah is Benjamin. With Judah you now also have a name change as well and that is "Jew". The name "Jew" comes from Judah or Benjamin. Now let's look more at Judah in Joshua 15:1-63, NKJV. If you read these verses it talks about the boundaries of Judah. Look at V.63, "As for the Jebusites, the inhabitants of Jerusalem, the children of Judah could not drive them out; the Jebusites dwell with the children of Judah at Jerusalem to this day." Judges 1:1-19 "This is Judah's land the Jewish State of Israel, because the Jewish state of Israel (Judah) has its own land that God has promised them. Numbers 14:22-24, NKJV, "Because all these men who have seen My glory and the signs which I did in Egypt and in the wilderness and have put Me to the test now these ten times, and have not heeded My voice, they certainly shall not see the land of which I swore to their fathers, nor shall any of those who rejected Me see it. But my servant Caleb, because he has a different spirit in him and has followed me fully, I will bring into the land where he went, and his descendants shall inherit it." Now as you read those verses remember that Caleb is from the tribe of Judah. The Jewish state of Israel (Judah) inherits that land. In 2 Chronicles 36:23 and Ezra 1, you will read that the house of Judah comes home (the Jews,) the one who God promised that land to, which is The Jewish state of Israel. When they named their State they wanted to name it Israel, but they didn't, if you look at the document to this day when they named their State it says the" Jewish state of Israel" and not just Israel. Did you know that there are more Jews living in New York then in their own land? They knew that they were all not of Israel, so they could not name it Israel and instead named it the Jewish state of Israel? If you also look at the whole book of Ezra it has nothing to do with the ten tribes which is the house of Israel. It is <u>all</u> about the house of Judah. Read it sometime, it is very interesting when you first get to the names of people that we will get into later. None of those names in Ezra have anything to do with the house of Israel but it is all about the house of Judah!

In the House of Judah are, Judah, Benjamin, and some Levites.

The name "Jew" comes from Judah or Benjamin. Look at the New Testament. You have Paul saying that he is a Jew, and is from the tribe of Benjamin, and with that he has claim to be a Jew. In Ester 2:5 it says that there is a Jew whose name is Mordecai and who is also from the tribe of Benjamin. If you are from one of these tribes you do have claim to be a Jew.

In 1 Kings 16, the word Jew is mentioned for the first time and it has to do with the House of Judah. Therefore Judah took on the nickname, "Jew", which is a contraction of Judah. Judah would possess Palestine, would speak the original Hebrew tongue, and Judah came to be a remnant of people, few in number. Judah (through the Lion of the tribe of Judah) would possess the royalty blessing and this entitled them to the lineage of the Messiah. The sign that was over Jesus head on the cross, <u>Latin</u>: *Iēsus Nazarēnus, Rēx Iūdaeōrum*) represents the Latin inscription which in English reads as "Jesus the Nazarene, King of the Jews" and John 19:20 states that this was written in three languages, Hebrew, Greek and Latin.

The house of Judah is the Jewish state of Israel, anytime you read in the Bible about Judah or the house of Judah, your mind needs to take you back to 1 Kings, Chapter 11 and now you are reading about the two houses and the Jewish state of Israel. When you read end times scripture on the House of Judah that is about the Jewish state of Israel. In Ezekiel 37 when the two sticks come back together to make one stick the House of Judah (Jewish state of Israel) is one part of that stick, the other stick is the House of Israel

The House of Israel

Who is the House of Israel? Now we have finished with the House of Judah, and learned in the book of Ezra 1, that they established themselves and we know them today as the Jewish state of Israel. The question now is where did the House of Israel go? They are the ten tribes who did not come back with the House of Judah. Here are some verses that will help us try to figure this out. I want you to read these so you get a better look at who the House of Israel is.

1Kings14:15 – Israel gets uprooted.

Zechariah 10:11 - They pass through the sea with affliction.

Hosea 9:13 – Ephraim gets planted in a pleasant place.

Gen 28:14 – They will spread abroad North, South, East and West, how far will they spread is unknown until Duet 33:17 which says, "Ephraim's territory is to the ends of the earth".

Gen 48:13-22 – Israel through Ephraim would possess the birth- right blessing from Jacob and Israel would have a name change. Israel would acquire their own land separate from Palestine. Israel would speak a new language. Israel would be as the sands of the sea. Israel would be lost to their heritage. Israel would become a company or Commonwealth of Nations. Israel (through Ephraim) would possess the birthright blessing and this entitled them to great wealth.

It is kind of hard to talk about the House of Israel without going into our next chapter because it does tie in a lot with Ephraim. If you also look at the two Houses, the House of Judah and the House of Israel, in John 1:11 NKJV, it says, "He (Jesus) came to His own (Judah) and His own did not receive Him."

Matt 21:43, NKJV, "Therefore I say to you the kingdom of God will be taken from you (Judah) and given to a nation (House of Israel) bearing the fruits of it". You can look these two up on your own, but again these scriptures tie in both with the House of Judah and the House of Israel. Read Hebrews 8:7-10 and Ezekiel 37.

Who is the House of Israel?

I believe that the House of Israel is America. But, I do want you to understand how these two houses split, making two houses. Now when you read in scripture about the House of Israel this is not the Jewish State of Israel, the Jewish State of Israel is Judah, or the House of Judah. Ephraim's blessing from Jacob kind of kicks off this thing with America.

Ezekiel Is a Watchman

Read Ezekiel 3:16-21. A watchman is a God appointed person who prophesied God's warnings to protect his people. Ezekiel sat with the people and identified with their pain as he waited patiently for God's Word to come to him. When God spoke, He made Ezekiel a watchman and told him to stay home and be quiet until he received the message to speak. His silence was a sign to the people that God was angry with them for rejecting His Word and yet Ezekiel remained faithful. It is a serious thing to be a watchman, for the destiny of souls is at stake. The watchman must be alert to every opportunity and must not be afraid to sound the alarm. False watchmen will have much to answer for at the judgment. Read Isaiah 56:10-12.

The beginning of the "American Covenant".

The House of Judah is related to the Jewish State of Israel. Can we also relate the House of Israel to America? History seems to indicate that the House of Israel migrated to America. John 1:11, (NKJV),"He came unto His own, (Judah) and His own received him not." This means that Judah did not want anything to do with Jesus.

Matthew 21:43 (NKJV), "Therefore say I unto you,

the kingdom of God shall be taken from you, and given to a nation bringing forth the fruits there of." If you also look at the New Testament, it is full of the disciples asking Jesus about either Israel or the House of Israel. The kingdom is going to be set up in the House of Israel (America). Look at the end times in Ezekiel 37:16-17, (NKJV), "Moreover, thou son of man, take thee one stick, and write upon it, for Judah, and for the children of Israel his companions: then take another stick, and write upon it, for Joseph, the stick of Ephraim, and for all the house of Israel his companions, verse 17, And join them one to another into one stick and they shall become one in thine hand." This means the House of Judah and the House of Israel will come back together at the end of all ends. Ephraim which is the 13th tribe gets the stick which is America.

I like what Hebrews 8 talks about with the new covenant; it says in verse10,"for this is the covenant that I will make with the house of Israel." Read the whole chapter of 8 though to get the meat of it.

Revelation and the Old Testament

Who was King Solomon's father? (King David). David is from the House of Judah, which is the State of Israel. The first covenant was between God and Moses. The Levites were the priests chosen to care for the temple and carry out the sacrifices and priestly duties for Israel. Jesus did not come to destroy the laws of the first covenant but he came to fulfill the laws of the first covenant. Because of David's bloody missions in his life, he was not chosen to build the Temple for God. Because David was a man after God's own heart, He was promised that his son would build the Temple, and through Solomon this was fulfilled.

Now when King David had an affair with Bathsheba she conceived a child, and he attempted to cover up the sin by having her husband come home and sleep with her to cause him to believe the child was his. David's plan did not work, and Uria had much nobler ideals in time of war, and refused to sleep with her. As you know, then King David had Uria stationed in the front lines and killed in battle. He then married Bathsheba and the child died shortly after birth. David was confronted about his sin by the Prophet and was told because of this sin, his house would be divided. Most of the tribes would be Israel, but only one remained from the tribe of Judah, thus two Kings. That was God honoring David for his great love of God's principles even though he failed with Bathsheba. So now we have two houses. The House of Israel, which is the State of Israel. And we have the House of Judah, also known as the house of David, the promised House of the eternal King who would be King forever and rule the world.

When Jesus became our ultimate sacrifice and died for the whole world to forgive our sins, a new covenant was established. This covenant has grace and mercy to cover the laws that are broken. This no longer applied just to the Jews, but to all people. So we have two groups of people now. We have the House of Judah, or House of David, which is Israel with the laws and sacrifices; and we have the group of people under the 2nd covenant, who were the Jews who accepted the sacrifice of Christ, and the gentiles who accepted the sacrifice.

When America was being established, George Washington, Like Moses, made a covenant with God. Israel and America are the only covenant nations among all nations, both born of God with Judeo-Christian principles. I believe Israel is the House of Judah and America is the House of Israel in prophecy.

In a Bible Study we have been looking at an over lay of the Tabernacle. We have been talking about the House of Israel, and the House of Judah referring to the inner court and outer court people. The outer court people are uninformed and biblically incorrect. They are the "beast" people. The inner court is where we want to be, protected, favored and blessed. In observing this in the Church of America, I understand the separation within the church in these matters. There are some who believe they are "spiritual" but they are in the outer court. Very few are making it into the inner court. Outer Court people do not want to be politically involved in stopping the things that bring down our freedom, liberty and moral system which God has given us. Our spiritual leaders are not talking against the people we vote into political offices, who favor the beast system. Therefore you get the outer court people who think they are following Christ, but in reality they are serving the Anti-Christ.

What is the "beast system"?

The One World order, the One World economy is the beast system. It's a group of United Nations, joined together with one thing in mind, to control and oppress. Its hatred centers on cultures and people groups associated with Christ, who it then seeks to control. It has an economic system with a long reach, which it uses to control and oppress. This is not a free market system, and you cannot buy or sell without its mark. George Soros, Obama, Bill Gates, Paul Allen, China, Russia, Patty Murray, Gov. Jay Inslee, and many more are on the list. We all need to be aware of these people. Most of them come in the name of the Lord, but they are in deception, so be aware of them. It has a legal system which creates its laws of governance, and these laws are carried out with the express purpose of control and oppression. There are no checks and balances in this system. It has a military police force for the enforcement of those laws. These are the same people who defy the Constitution. It's out to destroy the Bill of Rights and the Declaration of Independence. Also we see both Islam and Communism are oppressive systems, and are joining forces to establish a united front. These systems may not necessarily be anti-God but they are both anti-Christ. Look at Russia and Iran for an example. Communism alone is responsible for making more Christian martyrs between 1900 and 2000 than in all of human history leading up to that time. Is it any wonder that God would be against Gog? With them is Islam. Islam is at war (jihad) with all who they deem to be anything Christian or Jewish. Both Communism and Islam have two primary enemies. They are America and the Jewish State of Israel. Should Communism and Islam unite, the world would quite literally have the beast on its hands. In the words of Revelation 13 who could make war with it? Who do they both want to destroy? America, (the House of Israel) and the Jewish state of Israel (the House of Judah)".

This may be alarming to some of you; much of this could have been delayed or stopped at the pulpit. We need spiritual leadership that has integrity and courage and ARE WITHOUT FEAR for God's word.

A quote from **The Light and the Glory,** by Peter Marshall and David Manuel:

Chapter 7, Page 157.

By now, a farewell sermon had become a tradition, and it was preached by a stalwart young Puritan minister named John Cotton, whose star was also destined to rise over New England. He preached on 2 Samuel 7:10 (KJV): "Moreover, I will appoint a place for my people Israel, and will plant them, that they may dwell in a place of their own and move no more; neither shall the children of wickedness afflict them anymore, as before time."

: Go forth: Cotton exhorted," . . . with a public spirit." With that "care of universal helpfulness . . . Have a tender care . . . to your children, that they do not degenerate as the Israelites did . . ."

Samuel Eliot Morison put it thus: "Cotton's sermon was of a nature to inspire these new children of Israel with the belief that they were the Lord's chosen people; destined, if they kept the covenant with Him, to people and fructify this New Canaan in the western wilderness." And Cotton concluded his sermon:

What He hath planted, He will maintain. Every plantation His right hand hath not planted shall be rooted up, but His own plantation shall prosper and flourish. When He promiseth peace and safety, what enemies shall be able to make the promise

of God of none effect? Neglect not walls and bulwarks and
fortifications for your own defense, but ever let the name of the
Lord be your strong tower, and the word of His promise, the
rock of your refuge. His word that made heaven and earth will
not fail, till heaven and earth be no more.

Prophecy from Mel Jolley 6/18/16

Isn't it from the House of David that I told you the Lion
of Judah would come? Keep your eyes upon Israel and watch
and learn. I sent you a Lamb of peace and serenity, but you
slayed Him and rejected Him. I gave you a home land and
have kept my covenant with my people. When I sent you
out into the world to take the message, the covering of the
House of Israel went with you to build a new nation for the
people who believe in my Father. I gave you a covenant of
peace, serenity and liberty. I gave you boundaries from sea to
sea. I have showed you peace and liberty, but even there you
have rejected me. I told you that you would surely see the
day that the lion would lay down with the lamb in serenity
and peace.

I will not be rejected any more. Those who accept my
word have learned to submit to me and humble themselves.
They followed after my life and have kept My precepts all
the days of their life. Woe unto the nations that have fallen
by the wayside and have rejected the truth. For those people
had the Word of the truth and have rejected it for surely you
must know the days of judgement are upon you.

The Churches have been very silent on our Jewish
heritage. To better understand what is going on in the world
around us today, we must be learning about the House of

Judah which is the land of Israel and the House of Israel which is America. You will not find the word *America* in the Bible. However it is very plain to see when you read in the first book of Kings, chapter 11, about the ten tribes of Israel. America and Israel are both covenant nations under the same God. The House of Judah, in Israel, kept the laws. They lived under the covenant in the Old Testament. The House of Israel, In America observed the laws, but was living under "grace" in the New Covenant found in the New Testament. Both covenants are under the same God. Revelation12 tells us about the harlot, which is America. The other woman who delivered the child represents the House of Judah.

You may remember me speaking of two covenant nations; Israel and America. I would like you to see in this passage that I am sharing, about the destruction of all the things of Baal and the grove to see what happens when a nation turns its back against God's values, and then later repents and has to destroy the idoltry and objects of worship to false gods. I pray that all may come to a hunger for the Word of God. Read 2kings 23:1-4. The King sent for all the elders, men of Judah and inhabitants of Jerusalem, as well as the priests, prophets, and all the people, and read to them the book of the covenant that was found in the House of the Lord. The King made a covenant before the Lord to walk after the Lord and keep His commandments, testimonies, and statues with all their heart and soul, to perform the words of this covenant that were written is this book. All the people stood for the covenant. The King commanded Hilkiah, the high priest, to take out all the vessels of the

temple that were made for Baal, the grove and all the host
of heaven, and burn them in the fields of Kidron and carry
the ashes to Bethel.

Read Luke 24:13-21. The same day two of the disciples
of Jesus were walking to Emmaus and talking about
everything that had happened. As they were walking, Jesus,
who they did not recognize, joined them and asked them
what they were discussing. Cleopas asked Jesus "Are you the
only one visiting Jerusalem who does not know the things
that have happened these days"? Jesus asked "what things"?
They then told Jesus about Himself, how He was a powerful
prophet of God in word and deed. The chief priests and
rulers sentenced Him to death and He was crucified. The
disciples said, "We had hoped that He was the one who was
going to redeem Israel". They also said it was the 3rd day
since this happened. Look at Luke 24:21, NKJV, "we had
hoped that He was the one who was going to redeem Israel?"
(The Messiah)

Look at Acts 1:6, NKJV, "6 Then they gathered around
him and asked him, "Lord, are you at this time going to
restore the kingdom to Israel?" Restore the Kingdom to
whom? Israel! Now in the study we have done, who is Israel?
The ten tribes which are whom? America. Remember the
two tribes are Judah, and the Jewish state of Israel. The
problem is most people do not know these things so we kind
of stay away from it. This would make for a great pulpit
teaching if you ask me.

Also Jesus found His disciples and told them that they
will be guided by the Holy Spirit, make sure you listen
and receive it. Remember the story about Peter, John and

James? They were fishing and there was a guy standing on the beach and told them to throw the net to the other side; they did and they could not even pull it up because of all the fish they had. Yes that guy was Jesus and it was during His 40 days on earth after His death and resurrection. He also talked with them about the kingdom of God, "talk about being a fly on the wall that would have been very cool to hear. Things churches could be teaching their people!

CHAPTER SIXTEEN
Word of God

What is His name? Many do not know His name. Who is coming back?

Read Proverb 30:1-6

Sayings of Agur

It says in this proverb that someone weary can prevail. Even though you have no human understanding, wisdom, or knowledge of God! It then asks questions of who has gone up to heaven and come down? Who gathers the wind? Who has wrapped the waters in a cloak? Who has established the ends of the earth? What is His name and His son's name? Surely you should know that this is.......Jesus of course! This acknowledges that only God has gone up to heaven and back when Jesus ascended into heaven after He died on the cross and arose from the grave. He is our creator and has established all the dimensions of the earth! God has a son, and His son is Jesus! God's word is perfect and He shields those who love Him. Do not add to His words as He will prove you are a liar and will rebuke you!

Revelation 19:13 KJV

[13] "And He was clothed with vesture dipped in blood: and His name is called The Word of God". This is describing our Lord, Jesus Christ. Read Luke 6:27-31. Love your enemies. Do good, bless and pray! Turn the other cheek. Give to those who take and ask from you. If someone steals from you let them keep it. Basically do as you would have done unto you. It is my belief in these matters that many of us have been deceived by Satan, or the Leviathan spirit, by not putting into action what we learn from Proverbs and James. We should be good stewards of God's Word in all matters. We are not to be co-dependent in enabling people to continue in their way of sin. We have to rely on the Holy Spirit to guide us in all situations. God is not asking us to be a double standard or to be abused by the evil one. Use wisdom when applying the above scriptures to your life.

Read Luke 6:32-36. If you love those who love you or do good to those who are good to you, what credit is that to you? Sinners do that. If you lend to those who pay you back what makes you any different from a sinner who does that? Love your enemies, do good, lend without expecting repayment, then you will have a great reward and will be considered a child of God because God is kind to the wicked and the ungrateful! Be merciful as your Father is merciful!.

In the matter of lending and giving, God would have us to give. Do not lend unless you are willing to give it. You cannot expect all to pay restitution. This would be the heart of Christ to give, rather than lend. Lending can cause problems when the item lent out is not returned. Satan can use such a situation to cause problems in a friendship if one does not comply. Not everyone, including Christians, have the heart or mind of God.

In reading the book of Hebrews, I want you to keep in mind that God is speaking to a covenant nation that should know who their high priest is along with the leadership. I am sharing these particular scriptures in hope to encourage you to read the "rest of the story". Read Hebrews 5:10-14. Jesus was designated by God to be the high priest in the order of Melchizedek. In Hebrews, the people were slow in learning and did not try to understand. They should have been more advanced in their Christian walk and ready to be teachers, but they still needed to be taught the elementary truths of God's Word all over again! Their growth was stunted. They did not know the teaching about righteousness and were infants in their faith. They needed constant training in how to determine good from evil.

Hold your socks on for this! I believe in a good strong salvation message, but equally in a good strong UNCOMPRIMISED Word! I will say there is a time and place for the strong salvation message, but when we come together as brothers and sisters in the Lord to study His word, we are to dig much deeper and go beyond the simple message of the Gospel. We must go for the uncompromised word that truly does the teaching of our Heavenly Father's will. This is why it is so urgent to have a complete and thorough understanding of the "Old Testament". The Old Testament confirms everything that is in the New Testament. That is what will bring the New Jerusalem and the Bride of Christ to peace. When this happens, the church will be cleansed and Christians will no longer desire to be part of the world. Cleansing usually includes great loss, persecution, suffering and blood.

I find it interesting that I spoke on phony Christians at the nursing home Tuesday night. My text was taken from James 3:3-12. I think we who claim to be Christians need to forsake and lay aside all denominational dogma and focus on the true principles and values that God's Holy Word teaches us. Love each other as Christ loves the church which just happens to be those who accept His Word and not that of man.

It is ok for us to have a difference of opinion. In most cases we are saying the same thing but only using different wording or terminology. The most important thing is to identify evil for what it is. However this cannot be accomplished unless our spiritual leadership, as well as we, know the Word of God. Scripture tells us in 2Corinthians 6:17 (KJV):"[17] wherefore come out from among them, and be ye separate, saith the Lord, and touch not the unclean thing; and I will receive you." If Pastors and ministers cannot teach this from the pulpit for the fear of losing their 5013c or the fear of the Bible being "hate speech", we need to have the courage to stand on our own and move on with those who have their roots well planted in God's Word. It's by the Holy Spirit that we gain our strength; not by "conforming to the world".

I was talking to Larry, who is an acquaintance, after a memorial service and he asked me what church I was going to. My reply was God's church of course! I think there is a fallacy out there that people are believing that you have to be a card carrying member of a particular denomination or group in order to be a Christian. I feel the Word of God teaches us that we are to connect ourselves to like-minded people in Christ and His teachings. My true feeling is that as time goes on more people will be connecting to home churches and Bible studies. As it becomes more personal, they will be enlightened in the truth; and the hypocrisy and double standard of the church will become clearer to those who are seeking God's truth. The clear word is that you cannot serve two or more gods. You can't be progressive or liberal and be voting for those who want to legalize unclean things. God is moving people out of the brick and mortar denominations that don't teach or refuse to fight against immorality. When you surrender yourself to the Word of God, God starts to heal your mind to where you have some common sense. It is not a "God thing" to put little girls in locker rooms with men and boys, or using same bathroom facilities just as it is not of God to be teaching your child that homosexuality is the "norm" when the Word of God is clear about sodemy and having sex with their same sex. It is not of God to be teaching our children who are being raised up in His word, that its ok to pollute one's mind and body with substance abuse. God tells us to be of sound mind. It is not of God for us to be teaching our children that murder by "abortion" is ok when the Bible is clear, that God knew you even before you were knitted in your mother's womb! When you seek the Lord in all things the truth will matter to you. The same goes for when you are not seeking the Lord in all things, the truth is meaningless.

Read 2 Timothy 4:1-5 in you Bible. Here is a small scripture that most of us take no heed to. We don't know how to apply it to our lives. It will test us in our growth in the Word of God as well as our responsibility to Him. In this scripture we are charged to preach the Word. Be ready in season and out of season. We should convince, rebuke, and exhort with longsuffering and teaching. The time will come when people will not endure sound doctrine, but will follow their own desires and find teachers who will not teach the truth but fables. Be watchful in all things, endure afflictions and evangelize. Proclaim the message; be persistent whether the time is favorable or unfavorable; convince, rebuke, and encourage with the utmost patience in teaching.

Apostasy is coming! An abandonment of one's religious faith, political party, causes, or principles! Many professed Christians have no "ear" for the Word of God. They prefer religious entertainment and sermons that will tickle their ears instead of cutting their hearts. People will turn away from the truth; they will grow weary of the simple gospel of Christ. They will be greedy, and take pleasure in fables. People do this when they will not endure that preaching which is searching and to the point, and purpose. Those who love souls must be always watching and accept all the results of their faithfulness, and take all opportunities to make known the truth of the gospel of Jesus Christ.

God has many storehouses according to His Word. If you believe what the Word says, than you know the weather is ordered by God Himself. Here is a site to look up; it has 15 verses about God's store houses.

http://bible.knowing-jesus.com/topics/God-s-Storehouses

I know it is very hard to die to the flesh, however many of us who come in the name of the Lord fight this battle because we refuse to mature in the Word of God. We want to claim because we are living in the New Testament that we are under God's mercy and have nothing to fear. However this is not true. We must fear the Lord in order to have wisdom and through that God will show His mercy and grace on us individually. Gods' wrath and anger still is the same as it was from the beginning. Read in the Old Testament, "I am the Lord God and I change not". In the New Testament God said "Jesus is the same yesterday, today and forever". Jesus and God are the same as well as the Holy Spirit. This is called The Trinity. The Book of Revelation is all over the Old Testament. You will see that those who are without Christ have every right to fear God, but still the foolish do not! Remember also that there will be some who will say in that day, "Lord, didn't I prophecy in your name and do wonders in your name? And He will say "depart from Me, I never knew you!" So there are Christians out there who think they are saved and think they have nothing to fear, yet they are not going to make it! The fear of the Lord is the beginning of wisdom!

Something we don't often think about.

What is death? True death is the separation of God's presence and His Word. If you have noticed Christ did not die at Calvary. He gave up His spirit. We are made in the image of Christ. When we give up the spirit, our body which is the tent that our spirit dwells in begins to deteriorate. All of us will have eternal life. The question is where do we desire to spend that eternal life? Two choices, either with God in heaven; or our spirit cast into outer darkness, where there is no light of God and His glory, but just the darkness of the evil one, Satan.

Chapter Seventeen
President Trump

Inauguration of President Trump 2017

I was very pleased to watch the Inauguration of President Trump. I found it Christ centered and a cry to bring our nation back to the one true God, Jesus Christ. I was delighted to hear what President Trump had to share and say. I hope we all see fruit from what he shared from his heart. I was very pleased to hear the prayers of Godly ministers asking God to bring blessings and favor back to our nation. I cannot say the same for the news media. I was <u>very</u> disappointed and disturbed by the news media. The unprofessionalism, the stupid comments and criticism that was expounded on was as if it came from vipers themselves. It was as if they did not want a united nation or Christ centered nation. I prayed for good fruit and God's blessing and protection on our new leadership. I also suggested that all Christians pray for President Trump every day to listen to the Holy Spirit, make Godly decisions, and do God's will. Also, pray for his protection!

Well we made it through the inauguration and are experiencing Donald Trump, as our president. We have not seen martial law yet, nor a nuclear war. I believe we should give the credit where credit is due! God is still on the throne! I do believe that there are those out there who believe in the truth and are willing to change their life style to what is more conducive to God's Word. We have a long way to go in putting a stop to lies, knowing that a little lie is as bad as a big lie. This applies to all. God has given the watchmen, these charges:

Isaiah 62:6, KJV, "I have set watchmen upon thy walls, O Jerusalem, *which* shall never hold their peace day nor night: ye that make mention of the LORD, keep not silence,"

Ezekiel 33:6, KJV, "But if the watchman sees the sword come, and blow not the trumpet, and the people be not warned; if the sword come, and take *any* person from among them, he is taken away in his iniquity; but his blood will I require at the watchman's hand." The Lord wants us to always be prepared.

2 Timothy 4:2-4, (Holman Christian Standard Bible), ² Proclaim the message; whether it is convenient or not; rebuke, correct, and encourage with great patience and teaching. ³ For the time will come when they will not tolerate sound doctrine, but according to their own desires, will multiply teachers for themselves because they have an itch to hear something new.[a] ⁴ They will turn away from hearing the truth and will turn aside to myths".

It would be prudent to clean our own house first and get it in order before we clean up another nations' house.

When we passed over the 100 day mark with President

Trump, nothing had impressed me yet. I still felt he could be the man- child. There was no good in saying "what if", about Ted Cruz. He still would have been my first choice. However I felt for me and my family, we could rest secure in the arms of Jesus Christ, because we have the true foundation of God's Word to go by.

I read comments from my post on Face Book about the 100 day mark with President Donald Trump. I was very impressed with some of the replies. Some replies I was not in agreement with, but they were your choices and this is ok with me. I do not hate or dislike President Donald Trump! I can say the same thing for Ted Cruz. However I think we need to match the Word of God with people's actions. President Trump has been doing adequate work, in my opinion, and I have a "wait and see" attitude. I support him in those things that are good for America, and Constitutional, and uphold the principles of the Bible. Many of the things boasted about in the replies I got back, were not totally law or set in concrete yet. For those who thought that Ted Cruz was an illegal alien, as stated in the "fake news", this is not true! Do the actual research yourself. One other thing we all must understand is that we have to be honest with ourselves, honesty starts at home. All persons have dirty laundry which includes anyone we appoint or vote into office, including President Trump: and I thank all of you for your comments.

Obama leaving the White House

Obama was seen storming away from the West Wing after staffers from Donald Trump's transition team began preparing the executive offices for the new administration. On Trump's orders, one of Obama's most secretive rituals was reversed and all signs of it removed. For the past eight years, to appease Muslims working at or visiting the White House, silence has been ordered during the five times of Islamic prayer each day. In addition, prayer rugs and crescent moon symbols were available in several areas of the executive mansion to make Muslims more comfortable. The administration of Obama defended the practice by asserting that it also observed several other religious moments of silence and prayer out of respect, including a full "fifteen seconds" for Christianity on Sunday morning while a chaplain blessed a staff breakfast. None of the prayers is mandatory or led by a government official, which has allowed the administration to subvert 1st Amendment issues, but the obvious favoritism towards Islam, which is observed for Twenty-five minutes per day seven days a week, tells a story President Obama had denied for eight years.

President Trump

President Trump, who acknowledges that this country was founded by Christians and was built on Christian principles, removed all pagan symbols from the property unless they offered some historical significance. Only the cross in the White House Chapel remains for worship. President Trump doesn't see the need to provide prayer rugs and false idols in a house built by Christians. Washington, DC offers a diverse cultural center for the worship of any kind. You won't find any special considerations for Judaism or crucifixes to appease Catholics, either. There is a simple chapel with a single cross on one wall that is suitable for prayer by anyone. Our government doesn't need to be forcing prayer rituals down people's throats just so we don't "offend" people looking to blow us up. Patriots around the U.S. can rest assured that apologizing for our faith has come to an end.

Perhaps you have noticed how vulnerable some people's feelings are when two or more are sharing. Especially when it comes to political or faith based issues. This shows that one needs to have more maturity and growth in the way of the Lord. We as humans tend to forget that Christ loves everyone! However He does not allow sin. He has the capability of separating the two. I say this to give you an example: I appreciated the speech President Trump gave at the tree lighting and give him credit where credit is due. However this does not mean that I think he is walking on water. I was not pleased with Obama when he was in office, as well as other past presidents who refused to show their faith and the fruit of our Savior Jesus Christ. Perhaps we should look at ourselves individually, be objective with ourselves, and pray for those who are weak in Christ.

I want it to be known that I have not changed my principles or values. I did not vote for President Donald Trump or Hillary Clinton. I have maintained the principles and values given to me through God and the Founders. What is good about this is I know the truth in God's Word and what the outcome will be including the part that President Trump will play. I have accepted the fact that he is our President and I will pray for him daily as the scripture has instructed. We must be the best people we can be and choose the higher way, the God given way. "What would Jesus do"?

Many out there understand what has taken place with the United Nations voting against the United States and Donald Trump for the stand he took to move the embassy to Jerusalem. Many countries voted against America in this endeavor. I want it to be known that this is a very significant pivoting point in biblical history. My concern is for those who are not believers in what the Bible has foretold. These are apostate Christians who continuously challenge the Word of God because of their progressive and liberal thinking. However this will not change what the Word of God says. Those who understand biblical history should feel at peace knowing that God is still in control through this chaos and His Word is being fulfilled. In February of 2017, President Trump announced his decision to move the American Embassy capital to Jerusalem which shows the power of prayer and how God 'turns the heads of leaders!"

Chapter Eighteen
Priorities, Discipline, and Parents

Priorities

Responsibility and prioritizing are two things that I think "We" as Christians should have a full understanding of. Matthew 6:33, KJV: "But seek you first the kingdom of God, and His righteousness; and all these things shall be added unto you".

Warning! Do not become complacent in elected President Trump for all the answers! Be aware of who he has chosen to be his cabinet. These things are crucial for the direction that our nation will be taking. Man cannot supersede God's destiny and plan.

However as we have become new creatures in Christ by accepting Him, we have the responsibility of putting God first in all things. Husbands and wives are to put themselves second only to God. A healthy family makes for a strong community. God ordained priorities. Satan has stolen our priorities by discounting them and keeping us too busy to think. There are many times when we will have to put our families before our work, or going to church, and other church or Bible study activities. It is the leadership of each household's responsibility to see to it that the family is well balanced in the feeding of the Word of God as well as its application. Remember it is never too late to seek a new life for you and your family! God is the only one who can give you eternal life with Him.

As I am talking with people it is interesting to see how many of them don't even realize they are permanently separating themselves from their Savior, God. One of the most common phrases used is "I am too busy, or, "I just don't have time". You would be surprised how often these phrases come up in every day issues. Do you think something is wrong with their priorities? Let us open up our eyes to the truth about the Apostle Paul and the disciple that he was. As I have been reading through Paul's letters, especially Titus and Philemon, I come to realize what our church is lacking today, such as boldness with righteousness, and the ability to die to our flesh throughout the persecution of ourselves. There is a time proven adage that says, "As goes the leader, so goes the church." To be honest, we must see the suffocation and lack of the Spirit of God working in the body of Christ. Those who are called by His name will suffer persecution! We commend the church into your hands, Heavenly Father, and allow your Holy Spirit to release the church from the Leviathan spirit.

In Philemon, we see another example of Paul's boldness; He was appealing to Philemon on Onesimus' behalf for forgiveness. Read Philemon 1:15-17. "He was separated from you for a while, so you would have Him back forever. Not as a slave, but a beloved brother. If you consider me a partner, accept Him as you would me".

Read 1 Thessalonians 1:2-9. In these verses Paul is giving thanks to God for everyone, remembering their work, labor of love, patience and hope in Jesus. They were chosen by God, and the gospel had power through the Holy Spirit to save them. They received the word in affliction with joy and became examples to all who believe. They turned to God from idols to serve the true living God, and wait for Jesus from heaven, who raises the dead and delivers us from the wrath to come.

I came across a scripture the other day that most Christians are familiar with. I wonder if they understand the meaning and validity of this passage? Ask yourself what God is telling us here. I think it would behoove us to understand the importance of knowing His Word personally and be able to apply it to our lives knowing that our eternal life is of the utmost importance!

Treasures in Heaven
Matthew 6:19-21

Do not collect for yourselves treasures on earth where moths and vermin destroy; thieves can break in and steal. Store up treasure in heaven, where nothing can destroy and no one can break or steal. Where your treasure is, there is your heart.

Mel's Psalm 9

When I find myself slipping into darkness and I feel confusion coming upon me, and the spirit of the flesh fighting the goodness that's within; how far must I fall? I know that it isn't just what the world would call bipolar, or depression, or one of the other seventy dollar words, but it has to do with what I feed my spirit. I find myself needing to discipline myself in the way of the Lord, for He is my great shepherd and the Word that I stand on. He is the river that I lay by and drink from, that flows from the throne, and I shall never thirst. He is my bread of life. And when I find myself feasting on these things, I find myself rejoicing, and I say "rejoice in the highest"! While basking in His glory! My spirit is not brought down to the depths, but I am lifted up in His glory!

Written by Rev. Mel Jolley

Discipline

37 verses were found on Discipline. Not all are in this study. The Focus is to be disciplined to hear the voice of God through the Word of God. Discipline means training to act in accordance with rules. The discipline is God's Word in thought, word and action. From heaven He made you hear His voice to discipline you. On earth He showed you His great fire, and you heard His words from out of the fire.

-
- Job 5:17, NIV
- Blessed is the man whom God corrects; so do not despise the discipline of the Almighty.

- Psalms 94:12, NIV
- Blessed is the man you discipline, O Lord, the man you teach from your law;

- <u>Proverbs 1:7, NIV</u>
- The fear of the LORD is the beginning of knowledge, but fools despise wisdom and discipline.

-

- <u>Proverbs 3:11, NIV</u>
- My son, do not despise the Lord's discipline and do not resent his rebuke,

- <u>Proverbs 5:23, NIV</u>
- He will die for lack of discipline, led astray by his own great folly.

- <u>Proverbs 6:23, NIV</u>
- For these commands are a lamp, this teaching is a light, and the corrections of discipline are the way to life,
- <u>Proverbs 10:17, NIV</u>
- He who heeds discipline shows the way to life, but whoever ignores correction leads others astray.

- <u>Proverbs 12:1, NIV</u>
- Whoever loves discipline loves knowledge, but he who hates correction is stupid.

- •

- <u>Proverbs 13:18, NIV</u>
- He who ignores discipline comes to poverty and shame, but whoever heeds correction is honored.

- •Proverbs 15:10, NIV
- Stern discipline awaits him who leaves the path; he who hates correction will die.

- Proverbs 15:32, NIV
- He who ignores discipline despises himself, but whoever heeds correction gains understanding.

- Jeremiah 17:23, NIV
- Yet they did not listen or pay attention; they were stiff-necked and would not listen or respond to discipline.

-
- Jeremiah 32:33, NIV
- They turned their backs to me and not their faces; though I taught them again and again, they would not listen or respond to discipline.

-
- 2 Timothy 1:7, NIV
- For God did not give us a spirit of timidity, but a spirit of power, of love and of self-discipline.

-
- Hebrews 12:5, NIV
- And you have forgotten that word of encouragement that addresses you as sons: "My son, do not make light of the Lord's discipline, and do not lose heart when he rebukes you,

- <u>Hebrews 12:7, NIV</u>
- Endure hardship as discipline; God is treating you as sons. For what son is not disciplined by his father?

- <u>Hebrews 12:8, NIV</u>
- If you are not disciplined (and everyone undergoes discipline), then you are illegitimate children and not true sons.

- <u>Hebrews 12:11,NIV</u> No discipline seems pleasant at the time, but painful. Later on, however, it produces a harvest of righteousness and peace for those who have been trained by it.

- <u>Revelation 3:19, NIV</u>
- Those whom I love I rebuke and discipline. So be earnest, and repent.

To have discipline brings serenity and peace.

Days of Ezekiel and Jeremiah

I had dinner with a couple of other Pastors. While talking with them on different topics of current events it came to my mind that we are living in the days of Ezekiel and Jeremiah. I understand none of us will agree on everything. However it baffles my mind when there are those who brag "I led x amount of people in the sinner's prayer and they all were saved". I am of the opinion of how really foolish this sounds. The principles and values that the scripture teaches us should give us integrity through Christ and the

Ribbon of Darkness 137

Holy Spirit. This is why I have always said you can read the scripture and go to church constantly, but if the Spirit of God isn't there convicting us of our moral responsibilities we are a person without true integrity. Knowing this, I would like to encourage all of us to pray for those people, in the ministry, who need God's conviction, knowing that there is much more to salvation than just saying the sinner's prayer. We must take the responsibility of upholding our heavenly Father's principles and values. There is goodness in disciplining and teaching to help moral character and integrity develop.

I don't believe that God would have us choose between two or three evils, He has the right choice in mind for His people. When the wrong choice is made there are consequences to reap. There are a lot of people who should be and will be living their lives in fear for neglecting the knowledge of the Word of God. All of us need to understand change. Change is something that requires a renewing of one's mind and actions. When we come to the knowledge and wisdom, that there is a change required we should have the strategy and willingness to prepare and come to a greater one than ourselves to deliver us from evil. This means that we learn from our past mistakes. We restore ourselves to the truth and the light that God has given us. We then have the complete understanding that the relationship between man and God is a personal relationship, and we all come to Him in the same manner. Without persecution, trials and tribulation one cannot see the glory and the fullness of their Savior.

There are a lot of people who may come in the name

of the Lord, and say things without realizing that it hurts another person. We must come to realize that the Love of Jesus Christ is not a continuous pink cloud experience. However through diligence and correction with proper instruction, "discipleship," we are to grow in the way of the Lord. I say this because there are times when I personally have been hurt through this type of abuse. Someone saying that "it is easy for you to say" when your life is going so well for you without realizing that perhaps the other person has walked through the fire and have had times of tribulation as well as physical and mental wounds. I think this is what the scripture in the New American Standard Bible, Matthew 7:5 means. "You hypocrite, first take the log out of your own eye, and then you will see clearly to take the speck out of your brother's eye." In the application of using this passage we are able to see that one is as sick as we were, or perhaps still are, and need to focus on a solution before we can instruct some else in solving their issues.

Comments on Proverbs 28

(V21) Praise brought out the best in David but the worst in King Saul. Read (Sam.18:1-16) what does it do to you? Friends should be faithful to each other. But you also need to be loyal to family and neighbors, (V.10). You never can tell when you may need them or they may need you! Not everybody will become a close friend but do not get so exclusive that you neglect other people. "Flattery is not communication; it is manipulation."

As crime increases, the government must pass more laws and hire more people to enforce them. (V.2) When you break

God's law, you promote the wicked; when you obey His law you promote the righteous; when you obey His law you promote righteousness (V.4) and enable God to answer your prayers. (V.9) Read Romans 13 and see what God says about Christian citizens? Wicked rulers are like fierce animals (V. 15) who drive the righteous into hiding (vv. 12,28) This includes ignorant leaders and those grasping after money (V.16) The people in that day could not vote to replace leaders or correct laws, so all they could do was protect themselves. When laws and leaders are unjust, usually the poor suffer and the rich profit. But even a poor person can have integrity (V. 6) and understanding (V. 11) and faith that God will meet his needs. (V.27) is there someone you should help today?

Parents

Discipline is good parenting!

Proverbs 13:24, (NASB), "He who withholds his rod hates his son, But he who loves him disciplines him diligently".

Thinking of a New Year's resolution? Perhaps it would be nice to focus on family values, and teaching our children that the love of Jesus Christ and our eternal life are more important than a new car, house, or technical gadgets.

Gender is God's choice

When did "gender" become the choice of parents, or the government? Biblically, gender is God's choice. "I formed you in your mother's womb." Psalm 139:13.

Wouldn't it be prudent for those who are Christians to bring up their children in the way of the Lord? Proverbs 22:6 KJV: "Train up a child in the way he should go: and when he is old, he will not depart from it." Parents and Spiritual leaders should work together in these matters and encourage the youth to carry their principles and values by the way of the cross into whatever vocation they choose. The parents and the church should cleanse the text books to reflect the truth.

CHAPTER NINETEEN

Leadership and Community

Have the Courage of your convictions

It's my hope that you will follow me into 2Peter. We need leadership in general to have true grit. I'm thinking along the lines of Clint Eastwood, or John Wayne. This goes without saying our beloved Apostle Peter had this kind of leadership in 2Peter 2:2-4. The way of truth will be maligned because of sensuality and greed. Many will exploit with false words and they will be punished along with the angels who sinned and were cast into hell. I think you get my point. We need boldness in our actions and great discernment and prayer before we act. There is great deception out there as we apply these scriptures to today.

Definition of Love

I was asked what is true love? I answered with emotional tears coming from my heart; the answer is in the Word of God found in 1 Corinthians, Chapter 13. This passage defines what true love is. "I can have tongues of men and angels, the gift of prophecy, understanding all mysteries, all knowledge, and I can have all faith to move mountains, but if I don't have love, I am nothing. If I give all my goods to the poor, or give my body for sacrifice, there is no profit for me. Love suffers long, is kind, does not envy, is not haughty, is not rude, does not brag, is not provoked, thinks no evil, and does not rejoice in iniquity. Love rejoices in truth and bears, believes, hopes and endures all things. Love never fails. Prophecies, tongues, and knowledge fail, cease and vanish away. Faith, hope and love, with love being the greatest, abide together". This is the meaning of love!

Community

I'm a person of disability from birth. Through the years of my life I have seen many people who are in need. They are disabled or poor because of tragedy and have been in need. The church could have reached out, but they didn't. I have heard reasons why they didn't, and I feel there is a lot of negligence in the church which prohibits God's work being done in the community. The churches' negligence has worked negatively toward winning souls because people have turned to the church for help, but there was none. I have also heard people say that they can't' "afford" to go to church. Speaking from personal experience, because of my blindness, I have approached churches myself through the years and can honestly say that I got very little help where I have had to endanger my life to achieve some things that would only take a few minutes for a "sighted" person to do. I know it is not up to the Pastor to do everything! It is up to the flock, the membership, to reach out and help each other in the time of need and carry that responsibility of the body. What is your church body doing to solve these issues?

Also ask yourself has your congregation become a victim of the 5013C? Do you require some type of record or receipt for helping in your church? The point I am trying to make is if the body of Christ was truly doing the bidding of the Lord, for the "Church", we could certainly have a smaller government. I was speaking on behalf of the truly needy people who have the willingness to labor and earn their keep. Giving food and clothing is one thing, however, when a quadriplegic, cripple, or blind person needs maintenance done around their house, either inside or outside, so they can keep their family home, it's the obligation of the believers in Christ to step up to the plate without expecting to be paid or reimbursed, and wanting a greedy handout. It should come from kindness, goodness and mercy. We do it unto the Lord. I talked to other Christians about this topic and their reply was "times have changed." Indeed they have. We see less and less of the Lord now and more of "what we can get out of it", a cruise ship mentality and club membership attitude. Our mission is home first, then overseas missions. We should not have to depend on the government when the Lord wants us to do these things for each other as commissioned in His word.

Chapter Twenty-Three
Washington State

A part of me rejoices for living in this fullness of time, seeing the Spirit of God move. Yet a part of me grieves like if my Guide Dog passed away. I know I must press forward in speaking the truth and standing for what is right. God has shown us through His word, this is true. For too long, too many of us have been silent and have done absolutely nothing. Yet we call ourselves the church and Christians. I have yet to see the fruit in the Pacific Northwest. I am speaking of my home state, Washington. No, I will not give up prayer or being God's messenger.

The reality is that even those who come in the name of the Lord, saying they are "Christians" have consequences to pay for their deeds and actions. I say this to wake up those people who say they are Christians and think that there is no accountability for their actions. It has to start with the bride of Christ which is the true church. They need to take the authority that God has given them through His living word. As you may know I live in the greater Puget Sound area where it's apparent that those who come in the name of the Lord are hypocrites. Very few, who are in spiritual leadership will speak out and be willing to stand up for righteousness, holiness and truly represent Christ in the community. The spiritual leaders in this area and maybe even in your area, are too comfortable to change even for Christ. They continue to flirt with their sins and play church and avoid dealing with issues.

Works of the flesh

Read Galatians 5:19-21. "The works of the flesh are adultery, fornication, uncleanness, lasciviousness, idolatry, witchcraft, hatred, variance, emulations, wrath, strife, seditions, heresies, envying's, murders, drunkenness, revellings, etc. They who practice these things shall not inherit the kingdom of God".

Read Colossians 3:5. "Cease doing fornication, uncleanness, inordinate affection, evil concupiscence, and covetousness, which is a form of idolatry". Read 1 Corinthians 7:2, "Avoid fornication by every man and woman having one husband or wife. Are you hearing these warnings in the sermons at your church, or are you getting a "feel good about yourself" message? It grieves my heart to know that there are people who don't see the evil and anti-Christ movement alive and well in the Pacific Northwest area. I say this because they keep voting the same deviant reprobate minded people into office. The government is not God and can't replace God even though many want it to.

Read Matthew 7:22-23. "Many will say to me on that day, Lord, didn't we prophesy in your name and drive out demons and perform many miracles in your name? I will tell them that I never knew you! Get away from me, you are evil doers"! God is not a liar and He is not "politically correct".

He does not say "black lives matter", He says "ALL LIVES MATTER WITH CHRIST"!

I have observed the churches in my area and what is going on in Washington State and our nation. As long as those who call themselves the body of Christ remain obstinate, stubborn, and refuse to repent and change, the chaos will continue. You will see the prophecy continue to be fulfilled. You must understand that I believe the Word of God to be fact and not fiction. When the Lord says He reigns on the just and unjust He does just that. While the leadership and the church refuse to rally their followers to become new creatures in Christ, they cease stopping those unclean and unworthy people from getting into office, and end up voting them in. We have to be ready to face tribulation. We cannot continue to allow the abominations, blaspheme, and denial of Christ; and expect our nation to come back to God, and keep the Constitution, and liberties as a free nation. Satan has his powers that God has allowed to test those who believe in Christ to fight for righteousness. Those who are of God can truly testify to the fact that this nation is not the same nation that it was ten years ago. We are not the same Washington State that we were either. Our moral values and sensitivities to Christ have only declined. While our spiritual leadership refuses to rally, we, the true believers better learn to seek the Lord on our own behalf and make the changes ourselves.

Sports can be idol worship!

Coming back from the Doctor one morning we drove by the Shoreline Nazarene church. On their bill board, they had written, game date, September the 18th. I was astounded when my wife told me this! Here we are in the process of losing our liberty and freedom and our churches don't even stand for principles and values! All three branches of our government are so corrupted and they are so concerned about "game day"? Why do they support the Seahawks when the Seahawks have taken a stand to not honor our country by saluting the flag? The NFL has no business being political if the church can't be political! The church worships at the throne of sports. Sports are the modern day idol worship!

Live God's principles every day!

Matthew 4:7, (NKJV), "Jesus said to him, "It is written again, 'you shall not tempt the LORD your God." I am speaking of the Pacific Northwest as a whole. It wouldn't make any difference if we had ten million churches in Washington State, it is still up to "We the People" to change our life style. As you look at Washington State and see what our politicians embrace, what they pass and lobby for, or stand for in principles and values, you see how corrupt the State of Washington is. In Romans 12:2 it says "And do not be conformed to this world, but be transformed by the renewing of your mind, that you may prove what *is* that good and acceptable and perfect will **of** God". My question for us, who call ourselves Christians, how do we live God's principles in our everyday lives? The way we are continuing to live, we are not applying God's word to our lives or we would see change. We need to vote out the politicians who do not stand for our principles and values. Christians need to run for offices and use their God given talents to lead. Christians are not living up to their responsibilities to be active in the communities that they live in. Christians are not voting and are burying their heads in the sand because they can't find Jesus to vote for. I have heard so many excuses from Christians who choose not to vote. Christians who are not voting are choosing to let our freedom and liberty be taken away! Matthew 4:4 says: "we shall not live by bread alone, but by every word that proceeds out of the mouth of God". Romans 12:2 and Matthew 4: 4 are both NKJV.

Abortion

I am more than livid with the people of the State of Washington as well as people who call themselves Christians and who sit back and allow the abomination of abortion to take place. You have the blood of the innocent on your hands! You may not like it but you are the vipers in the Church! You are totally guilty of refusing to hear the Word of God when science, medicine, and the Word, have clearly showed you the beginning of life! You refuse to be enlightened and you stay in the ignorance and the cess pool of your sin! I am totally disgusted with those people who force our insurance companies to participate in this sin and abomination against our free will. This is totally "UNCONSTITUTIONAL" folks! Where are the Christian lawyers and representatives of the Christian people? You stand guilty for doing nothing!

My prayer is that the Holy Spirit would move on those people who have their Constitution, Bill of Rights, and the Word of God, as their compass, such as the Black Robe Regiment group, Freedom Fighters, Constitutionalists, who would confront their churches and work with them. They need to proactively restore our Christian culture and heritage. It has to start with the Body of Christ.

Governor debate

I watched the Washington State Governor debate. Bill Bryant impressed me. He seems to be a man of accountability and is for small government. He wants communities to be responsible for their own communities. I was impressed by his plans of action to resolve our problems in the state such as mental illness, education standards, and funds being spent and accounted for. I cannot say the same for Jay Inslee. Jay Inslee has lots of pipe smoke dreams about raising funds by taxing to solve every problem by running our state further in debt. All of his solutions are entitlement fund solutions and socialism for all while pricing the middle class out of the state by taxing on fuel, and for the school programs. He wants to raise more taxes to handle traffic and funding drugs for addicted people. All the time the property taxes are going up. There has been no accountability for mismanagement of funds for our tax dollars.

Concerning the results of the voting ballots in Washington State:

Until some people realize the progressives and the liberals are in both parties, we will have the same viper mentality, unless they have a renewing of their minds by God. For those people who live in Washington State, just research yourself and take a look at who keeps pumping this poison into our state. Look at western Washington and King County. Who keeps voting for Patty Murry, Jay Inslee, Maria Cantwell, etc.? It's the anti-Christ spirit.

A dirty little secret in the State of Washington that most people don't check into:

This is about nursing homes and care facilities. I am speaking as a minister who visits nursing homes on a regular basis, once or twice a week. Most of them are grossly understaffed with certified nurses, therapists and aids. It usually will take the patients full social security check each month. The cost is staggering compared to the care that they get. As a minister, it appalls me to see this gross abuse of our fellow brothers and sisters being routinely neglected on a daily basis. We see bed sores, neglect of medicine given in a timely manner, not being seen by a professional doctor when needed, neglect of hygiene, toilet issues, and clean clothing and poor eating issues. It's about time we call the States' ombudsman's office and DSHS to report this neglect; we also need to notify our Senators and Congressman to try to insist they put a stop to this abuse.

Some people have hired professionals to come in to the nursing facility to care for their loved ones; however this adds extra cost for care which most people cannot afford. Some people feel that it is more work caring for their loved one in the nursing facility than taking care of them at home because of the daily trips which can be at least four times a day to make sure they are properly cared for. Also the staff becomes dependent on the people hired by family to do the work, and you are actually paying for double care which you are definitely not getting.

Death Penalty in Washington State

I would like to remind those who are supporting the end of death penalty in Washington State, that this is evil talking to your heart, it is not mercy. I am of the opinion that the Word of God is clear on this issue. This is an issue of Justice. Must I remind the people that Jesus Christ Himself was an innocent man who was executed and by His execution all people are eligible for salvation? Remember it was Christ's shed blood that provided salvation! This could only happen by dying on the cross, which was the capital punishment in those days. We live in such an evil society because we have not been upholding the Christian-Judeo laws that God Himself gave to us. Our prisons are overwhelmed with the worst of the evil because of the failure of the Department of Justice (DOJ) which has not followed the letter of the law. This has nothing to do with getting revenge but has everything to do with what is just. We have watered down the punishment system to the point where God's law has no reverence. Whoever commits a capital crime regardless of their age will not and cannot be a repeat offender once they face the death penalty!

Initiative 1433

The initiative 1433 Passed. It is big government crushing and controlling the masses by raising the minimum wage. It has no place telling people what the pay scale should be.

This is some more of that entitlement BS society poison. One more thing to prove how corrupt the State of Washington is!

Minimum Wage?

When it comes to equal pay, there is something that needs to be mentioned. I am not for entitlement or special interest groups. If we would follow God's principles and values we would be fair to all. I say this because as a disabled person from birth I have never seen one working day in my life when I experienced "fair pay". Honestly it does boil my blood when I hear women screaming for equal pay and other special interest groups doing the same when not one word is being said to advocate for the disabled. This has been a problem since time began. People need to get a life with Jesus Christ to make things right for all!

Initiative 1491

Be very careful about these initiatives. 1491 is written in a back handed way to strip us of our gun rights by doing it in the name of "safety". Use common sense when looking at these initiatives it is just another way to take your freedom away from you.

How the Evil anti-Christ establishment brings down the USA.

It could have started before Woodrow Wilson, Theodore Roosevelt, LBJ, Nixon, Jimmy Carter, the Bushes and the Clintons; but I want to remind us as we continue reading this, where was the Christian church? You have your local media such as in the Seattle area, KOMO, KING, KIRO, and their affiliates as an example of how Special interest groups are clamoring for their rights and political correctness, with the abuse of the usage of discrimination. One of the hot topics such as the nudity bicycle ride for summer solstice in Fremont was under the banner of "art". Is this something that we want to take our little children to? Really? Bathroom policies are another topic. Bathroom policies in public areas and schools, with an open door policy, provides for perverts to gather in the interest of human rights and promotes tolerance of unacceptable behavior by the majority. The ignorance of our society does not understand that in the book of Genesis, God created Adam as man, Eve as woman for companionship and being a sexual mate for procreation. Special interest groups have perverted this. I haven't touched such organizations as Green Peace, Environmental special interest groups, which are designed to tear down the economy and an attempt to break America's freedom of being independent from other nations. There are Special human interest groups that are designed to cause division amongst races and disabilities, ADA, (American Disabilities Act) to cause hatred, anger, and class systems which promote sheltered workshops, slavery, and ghetto mentality all in the name of special interest and human rights creating diversity and entitlement. Where was the church when it should have been challenging its shepherds "leadership"? Then we have the Politicians who didn't understand the biblical principles. God covered all of these issues in His word. It was the church and the shepherds who chose to allow this to happen when they took Christ out of the school system by denying the usage of the Bible and prayer all in the name of sensitivity and special interest groups that make "a diverse society". That is America's downfall of a broken covenant! Do your children know these things? When the church ceased to face these issues and neglected to teach how to rebut against them, it became an evil cancerous beast!

I need to share this. My heart goes out to Washington State and especially Seattle, Seattle City Council, King County and Olympia and the political leadership. I pray that you would all come to Christ with true repentance in your heart with fear and trembling before the Lord for surely you know there is a heaven, and a hell. But there are those who pray for you and love you, none more than King Jesus, to stop this insanity and blazing the trail to the gates of hell. There is a price to pay and for those who don't heed to His Word, they will feel His wrath. Some will call this an act of nature, but in your heart you know it's the act of God!

LGBT, Homosexuality, and Gay Marriage

The LGBT is one of the strongest movements in our nation right now. It has a very loud voice in the State of Washington and is responsible for the LGBT rights, gay rights and gay marriages being legalized. Public bathrooms are becoming unisex bathrooms and there is no regard for children and their safety from pedophiles who hang out in these places. If you are a Christian of any kind, and especially in leadership, your denomination and particular church group should be doing everything possible to defeat this evil that is confronting our nation and states. You should be working jointly together to oppose the wickedness of Satan or Anti-Christ. Just by the few things that I have been posting about LGBT and Sharia Law as well as Islam, it doesn't seem that there are many Christians who are willing to put the effort and extra time in to actually putting a stop to these programs. All of them oppose the Word of God. It may be ok to have the freedom of religion, this I can agree with however, it does not mean at the cost of Christianity and God's Word. I am saddened to see that more people are not doing something to oppose the flying of the Gay pride rainbow flag and asking for equal time for the Christian flag. I think it's beyond the point of no return when it's flown in your face everywhere. It's a total abomination to Christians and Christ. Those who call themselves Christians are just as guilty when they remain silent.

Sodom and Gomorra

We can see how much we have fallen into deception since the founding of America. We have heard of Sodom and Gomorra and the abomination that brought them down. In chapter 19, of Genesis, two angels appearing as men entered Sodom at night. Lot saw them and offered them housing. Before they went to bed, all the men of Sodom, young and old, surrounded the house. They called out to Lot, "'Where are the men who came to you tonight? Bring them out to us, that we may have sex with them." When Lot refused, they attempted to break down the door and forcibly have sex with these two visitors.

Sodom and Gomorrah were cities known for their many sinful actions, including homosexuality and even the attempted same-sex gang rape of visitors; and it had fewer than ten righteous people. God condemned their sin and brought judgment upon the cities, sparing Lot and his two daughters. Lot's wife disobeyed while fleeing by looking back at the city and died, turning into a pillar of salt. This makes me wonder how many righteous people we have in our cities. It's obvious that God is patient and merciful with us.

By the time Lot reached Zoar, it was morning. Then the LORD rained down burning sulfur on Sodom and Gomorrah and He overthrew those cities and the entire plain, destroying all those living in the cities and also the vegetation in the land.

This makes one wonder why our spiritual leaders and leadership of our government keep tempting the Lord our God when the scripture says in Matthew 4:7, KJV, "Jesus said unto him, it is written again, Thou shalt not tempt the Lord thy God".

For all you "Gay Prideful People"

I would like to bring something to your attention that deals with the "rainbow". You might want to consider that what you are doing is blaspheming and causing dissention to those who are following Christ. Read Genesis 9:8-17. For your information, I will refer you to what God said to Noah and his sons. God said that He would establish His covenant with them, and their descendants after them, and with every living creature such as the birds, livestock, and wild animals; all who were in the ark, and every living creature on the earth. The Lord promised to destroy the earth by the water of the flood, and never destroy the earth by a flood again. God said the rainbow would be a sign of the Covenant made between Him, you, and every living creature on the earth for all generations to come. That means forever! Every time the rainbow appears, God will remember His covenant. God told Noah that this sign of the covenant is established between God and all life on the earth. It speaks of the covenant that God made with the earth and its people. It had absolutely nothing to do concerning "pride" or being "homosexual". It was a promise that God would never destroy the earth again by a flood. You won't hear this truth spoken in your House of worship because it is not "politically correct". It is "righteously right" though!

Mayor debate

We had a mayor debate on King 5, Seattle, WA. There were six candidates. Later we found out that Mayor Ed Murry was guilty of being a pedophile. He was well known for being a "Gay" mayor. In saying this, I realize that this is his choice in life. However we as Christians have to learn to die to the flesh daily. This means dying in all choices that we make. That is the reason why it is so critical for us to constantly be judging current events by God's Word. This has to be our number one priority, if we want to continue to have any assemblance of the freedom that our founders and our Heavenly Father have given us. I prayed that this election for mayor would be the beginning of a new direction founded on God's values. We don't need to be catering to the sins of the flesh any longer! It's our responsibility as

Christians, each one of us individually, to voice our concerns by the ballot, or through city hall, or whatever means it takes. If not we are as guilty as those who we point our finger at and murmur about.

One might look at their own area; for instance, in Seattle, WA, the city council felt ready to have a transgender member. The people in Seattle elected mayor, Ed Murry, who condoned sodomy and who is a blatant professed homo- sexual. He saw nothing wrong with his lifestyle.

When will God's people say enough already? During his short time as mayor, Ed Murray was asking for the taking down of all confederate statues and monuments! The Bible tells us to not remove the ancient landmarks. We can't change History! Proverbs 22:28, KJV, says, "Remove not the ancient landmark, which thy fathers have set." God's people have been warned and this is happening all over our country by ungodly people who are doing the evil work of Satan to destroy the heritage of America as well as our Christian values!

The Governor of WA State condones these same activities by the sheer fact of wanting rights for all, even if it goes against principles and values. The same goes for the church. The fact is true that we serve a merciful God; however this does not negate His wrath or rejection of those who blatantly ignore His word. A true Christian would not be voting and condoning these activities!

The people of Seattle elected a new mayor. Ed Murry was chosen but because he is a gay pedophile, and got caught, he resigned and a lesbian attorney, Jenny Durkan was elected as mayor in his place. There are other candidates running for other offices. This is the time when we need to be searching our heart, and asking what would Jesus do? WWJD? We have already seen what happens when we compromise our values as well as our stewardship to the word of God. We need to be consistent and proactive in our discipline when it comes to these matters.

June is gay pride month

You probably know that June is gay pride month (LGBT). I am wondering how the spiritual leaders in my area feel about more people turning out for LGBT events then they do for Christian events.

Governor Jay Inslee raised the rainbow gay pride flag over the capitol in Olympia WA, to honor gay pride events. However, according to Scripture in the Bible, there is no pride in being homosexual or gay. It is called sin and abomination. How often does our governor, or any governor, raise the Christian flag above the capitol to honor our God, in whom our nation is founded, and in God's principles and values? And what about those men and women who believed in Jesus Christ and died for our nation?

I want you to think about something. How can one have a pure heart and justify total blasphemy and abomination? Notice through Gay Pride month how many churches are displaying the rainbow flag. Other places display the flag also. How can one even consider themselves part of God's family and know and understand the Word of God, yet still participate in this deviate blasphemy? It takes a reprobate mind. We understand the rainbow was a covenant given to the people after the flood in Noah's time as a promise that

God would never destroy the world in a flood again. This is an example of how the Leviathan spirit has taken covenants that we have made with God and perverted them. This shows me how many spiritual leaders refuse to take action and apply it with God's Word. There are very few leaders who will sound the trumpet. Anyone upholding the rainbow flag is participating in idolatry!

Bakery in Oregon

Lust is a peculiar strong weapon that Satan uses in our lives, even against those who are grounded in God's Word. We have to be constantly aware of this tool of Satan. I am sure that the Apostle Paul was very aware of this when he cried out that he must die to his flesh daily. Please refer to Galatians 5:24 and Romans 8:12-13. If any of us are aware of our spiritual walk with Christ we can see how this lust demon has infected all aspects of our world, not just in the government, but in the arts and entertainment and equally in the church. My heart grieved when I heard the news that was brought down to the bakery in Oregon for their morale stand against baking a wedding cake for a "gay wedding". I grieve for the judiciary system that we have in this nation that is blinded to the sin of lust. However for those who remain strong in God's Word, and do not placate or feed into this, which is co-dependency; we shall remain in God's grace.

My plea to "True Believers".

How do you feel about the town or city where you live? It is very frustrating as an American citizen living in Seattle, WA. As Seattle goes, so King County and the state go because the immorality is so embedded into our government. The traditional Bible believer does not stand a chance, when our local town and state government promotes immorality amongst the youth in the school system, and glorifies same sex marriage and homosexuality, by painting rainbow cross walks on the streets and glamorizing it with parades and festivals. When it comes to the Bible Believers and the sacred things that we stand for, such as "In God we trust", Prayer, the Cross, and just the word "Christmas", to openly display these things in the public square, as well as the school system, is vehemently opposed.

God's Wrath against Sinful Humanity

Read Romans 1:18-33. God's wrath is being revealed against all godlessness and wickedness of people who suppress the truth. God has made the truth plain to them and people are without excuse! They knew God but did not glorify or thank Him having futile thinking and dark foolish hearts. They forsook the glory of the immortal God for images like mortal humans, birds, reptiles and animals. God delivered them over to sinful desires in sexual impurity by degrading their bodies with each other. They exchanged the truth about God for a lie and worshiped and served created things rather than the creator. God gave them over to shameful lusts. Men and women chose unnatural sexual relations, preferring their own kind for partners. They did not retain the knowledge of God so God gave them depraved minds and they did what they should not do. They were filled with wickedness, evil, greed and depravity. They have envy, murder, strife, deceit, and malice. They are gossips, slanderers, God-haters, insolent, arrogant and boastful, they invent ways of doing evil; they disobey parents, have no understanding, no fidelity, no love, and no mercy. Even though they know that people who do these things deserve death, they do them anyway and approve of it for those who practice these wicked things. These things will continue to bring destruction to our nation. Those ministers who do not warn about this behavior will be held accountable by God.

Prayer Rally in Olympia with Franklin Graham

This was the believers' opportunity to join together from all over the State of Washington, at the Prayer rally in Olympia WA on June 29, 2016. It happened at noon. To show up in mass numbers as people in unity for God's principles and moral values was wonderful! We went to humble ourselves before the Lord, and repent of our sins. We need people of like minds to pray for restoration of our nation and Christian -Judeo heritage. Sadly, but true, more people turned out for the Gay Pride Parade then to unite together and seek God.

It didn't surprise me that the Gay Pride Parade and other related events had such a large turnout. However, my question is where are the spiritual leaders of the western part of Washington State with their spiritual leadership? Why is the Pope apologizing to the gay community for the Church? Why does he apologize for God's word? I thought Christians all serve the same and one true God and accept the Bible to be the absolute truth. I don't understand why they can't work together and put on a Christian event that lasts for seven days and fly the Christian flag on the space needle and on top of the Capital in Olympia. The Christians use to have a parade, but they had to stop it because the gay community found it offensive. I want it to be known publically that I have talked with many ministers of different denominations about this. There is NO interest what so ever! This truly shows the lack of seriousness that the church is displaying about salvation and protecting their sheep. This grieves God's heart that the church compromises on ALL the abominations listed in Romans 1, done in the name of Love! Remember Pride was the sin that cast Satan into hell. The church does not understand what love is, and it does not have boundaries anymore. This kind of leadership is leading masses straight into hell by ignoring sin. This is why elections are so important. There seems to be no difference between the church community and the world community. They live the same.

The anti-Christ movement seems to be constantly over powering Christians in their own country, America. This became real evident to me on June 25th when over 200,000 heathens turned out for "Gay Pride" and the local media was in your face about it all week long! I bet you will never see the day in Seattle that you will see over 200,000 people turn out to support Christian rights. With that in mind I would like to suggest a couple of DVD's that might help you on your research on Islam. "Islam and the Bible", by Wallid Shoebat; and "Chrislam exposed", by Pastor Shahram Hadian. More material is available through their websites. The irony in this is that Islam does not accept homosexuality but are in agreement with the LGBT community who are against

Christians. They both are against Christianity. We believers need to share positive support of God's Word when we see it posted on social media. If we believe it, we should share it and support those events that are truly upholding the uncompromised Word of God. By reposting you are allowing more people to see the truth.

Chapter Twenty-Four
Warning

"A Warning against Hypocrisy"!

Read, Matthew 23. The Teachers of the law and the Pharisees sit in Moses' seat. Jesus said, "Do everything they tell you, but do not do what they do! They do not practice what they preach. Everything is done for people to see. They look religious in appearance; love the place of honor at banquets, and most important seats in the synagogues. They love to be greeted with respect and called Rabbi by others. Don't be called Rabbi, for you have only one teacher, and you are all brothers. Don't' call anyone father on earth because you have one Father in heaven. The Messiah is your instructor. Those who exalt themselves will be humbled and those who humble themselves will be exalted".

We better take this seriously! There are many spiritual leaders who are not applying this today as we see the falling away of the church. Read the Seven woes in the part, "Teachers of the Law and the Pharisees", in Matthew 23. The truth speaks for itself. If you feel offended maybe you should ask yourself why. The spirit of God brings redemption to those who ask. For you know I am speaking the truth when I say this, many of us are guilty in not taking a stand in things for Christ; especially when it comes to our freedom and liberties.

Ezekiel 33:6, (KJV),"6 But if the watchman see the sword come, and blow not the trumpet, and the people be not warned; if the sword come, and take any person from among them, he is taken away in his iniquity; but his blood will I require at the watchman's hand."

Many of us allow the evil one to steal time away from us by not doing the Lord's work. He keeps us away from God's living word, so that the Holy Spirit cannot speak to us. I am speaking about those things that are not denominational or political party issues. However I will say I am speaking about those things that are right in Christ. There are people of reprobate mind in all sectors.

Read Ezekiel 33:17-20 in your Bible. There are those among us who will say we are called by God's name to minister or speak for Him. We are not being honest with ourselves or others if we are seeking out our own pleasure and popularity.

Commentaries on Luke 11: 39-44

Read Luke 11:39-44. There is an urgent code blue alert concerning the House of Worship in America. Please bear with me as I explain. Look at Luke 11:39. The cup referred to is the church. It looks great from the outside but on the inside it has a cruise ship mentality, casino atmosphere, complete with a rock festival and coffee shop feeling. As long as you are generous to the poor, you are in good standing with the church; your offerings deliver you from sin. It is easy for you to tithe your money yet neglect being righteously right and neglect Aaron's rod which happens to be in the Ark of the Covenant. You lack the love of God because there is no obedience or righteousness established. You need to establish righteousness first, follow up with your generosity and giving, and other good deeds. You love to be honored and recognized in Church with the "Donald Trump" mentality. You place your trust in the board, instead of the Lord. On the road to heaven your ideals and goals are traps to fall into and land on the road to hell.

I think we need to be of strong character to adhere to the uncompromised word of God unapologetically! And to those who are offended because of the conviction of the Holy Spirit "so be it". That's where the Lord wants them. Let's all read the Word of God with the eyes of the Holy Spirit.

We have come to a time when few are willing to renew their life style with a total commitment for Christ. Those who do will be mocked and persecuted for their choice, because they are the minority. Too many are willing to take the easy road and the broad path to pleasure as we continue our journey to entitlements and silencing the freedom of speech for the believer yet condoning and voting for progressives. Our nation is going the way of the world which is not God's way. The best thing that we can do is to pray for one another and ask God to open our minds.

Mainstream Media

It is amazing how the main stream media has become such a perversion of truth and a powerful tool for those who are anti-Christ oriented people, who choose to destroy

Americans and their lives. What is even more disgusting are the people who say they come in the "Name of Jesus", and don't even fight back with their dollars, opinions, and voices. I only know of two sources that will give me a balanced view of the news, they are CBN and The Blaze. CNN, Fox news, and the whole gamut of others are scandalous trash.

A Velvet Revolution is going into an iron fisted revolution

The South Dakota and Nevada poles, in my opinion, reflected that the people were very angry and were allowing anger to distort their good judgement. Combine that with the super delegate votes and this would cause an explosive situation. This is why we the people need a clear understanding of what the real progressive movement is, which is beyond being a "liberal". Right now our nation is "Crony Capitalism", which is close to being progressive socialism, which is one step from Communism. Is it obvious that we are in a "velvet revolution"? Now and within the next ten years we could be in a full fledge iron fisted revolt. I know speaking as an American citizen from Washington State; it looks like its full throttle ahead!

Slippery times

Accountability starts with you "at home, and at church. Let's not forget our destiny. "The shining city on the hill", that President Reagan talked about, can be achieved at a cost. Just as our destiny will be achieved at a cost; Scripture says "on earth as it is in heaven". How great would it be to see people standing up with full battle gear on and the "Word of

God" coming out of their mouths with a two edged sword in their hand, to slay the "Goliath's" of today? God has given us knowledge on how to replace corrupt leadership in our society. The church needs to bring this Word forth to the believers. We must be prepared in all things because when we become too busy pleasing ourselves, and not being conscious of what God would have us do, that is when Satan comes in to devour us as individuals and as a nation.

To those politicians of a depraved mind, let it be a warning unto you. Those who do not believe the truth shall not inherit the kingdom of heaven. I know this to be true because I believe the Bible is the Word of God.

John 14:6, NIV, Jesus answered, "I am the way and the truth and the life. No one comes to the Father except through me".

Matthew 5:37, KJV, "But let your communication be, yea, yea; nay, nay: for whatsoever is more than these cometh of evil." This is given as a warning to those who legislate sin to sanctify it.

Read Joshua 24:19-27, "Whenever you choose to serve other gods", Joshua told the people, "You cannot serve the Lord. He is holy, jealous and will not forgive your transgressions and sins. If you forsake the Lord to serve strange gods He will turn to hurt and consume you". The people said they would serve the Lord. Joshua told the people, "You are witnesses against yourselves that you have chosen to serve the Lord". They agreed they were witnesses. The people said they would serve and obey God's voice. Joshua made a covenant with the people that day and set them up with a statute and ordinance in Shechem. The words were written in the book of the Lord. Joshua took a great stone and set it up near the sanctuary of the Lord and said, "behold, this stone shall be a witness unto us, for it has heard all the words of the Lord which He spoke to us, and it shall be a witness to you lest you deny God". When I came across this passage in Joshua, it was as if the Lord was speaking to me saying, "We the people" need to take these words as a warning for America, which is a covenant nation like Israel.

It is the wise who know and are preparing for battle. The battle that we are fighting will be amongst ourselves. For you see perversion and evil have become the norm to the point where the church can't even make up its mind where the boundaries must lay, even while they have the truth, the Bible, in the palm of their hand! The next step will be for us to accept "pedophilia". When we look at the caliber of the people that we are accepting into leadership our standard is so low you can't even see God's hand in it. The majority is accepting evil and satanic things. The time is coming when it will be the remnant and the righteous among us who will say, "It is enough!" I find it blasphemy when those people who call themselves, "The Church," have sat back for so many years happy to remain silent, but this too has been written in God's word. This is why we have to educate and prepare ourselves individually and rise up against evil and fight this battle. Read Romans 13:11. Understand the present time for the hour has already come for you to wake up and realize that our salvation is nearer than we ever thought!

Diversity and Tolerance

We as Christians need to use caution with the words "diversity" and "tolerance". These words are being used to destroy a Christ- like way of life. They are not doing anything to win souls for Jesus Christ. They are being abused and used as a mask to disregard the truth and are sadly mistaken for compassion. God loves all people. He died for those who would choose Him by repenting and walking away from their sinful nature. The ones who did not accept His forgiveness and blood- sacrifice He could not die for because they had a choice to accept Christ or reject Him. That is clearly everyone's choice. They chose to reject Him. There is nothing more to be done about that. It's like one asking a believer to embrace a serial killers way of life and just let him continue killing people while fellowshipping with those who believe killing people is a sin. How can the two agree? Is this compassion? yes; but tolerance? What part of sin should be tolerated? Sin that has been repented of! So sin must be put away for the sake of Christ who laid His life down and paved the way and example for us to follow as believers. There will always be those who will justify themselves right into hell. As a believer in Christ, as much as it grieves us, we must allow them to have that choice.

There have been a few of us for the last ten years or so, who have warned that this kind of action would be happening in our nation's capital. We are sitting on the brink of becoming a Marxist nation. Right now as you are reading this, the Republican and Democratic Parties both are negotiating on how to compromise the Constitution. This is exactly why I have been preaching the last several years that our spiritual leaders need to stop playing games with the Anti-Christ establishment and make a stand for God and the Constitution! But will they do it? The answer is in the scriptures. Intuitively I know there are people who will never believe that the Bible is the inspired Word of God. However I feel that I need to put out a warning to those people who call themselves Christians and come in the name of the Lord, especially those in leadership positions in the government, as well as in the body of Christ. Here is a scripture I want to share with you. Isaiah 5:20 (NKJV),"Woe to those who call evil good, and good evil; "Who put darkness for light, and light for darkness; Who put bitter for sweet, and sweet for bitter"! If we have a working relationship with Christ much is expected of us. We are held to a higher standard. Many of us see the hypocrites, vipers, and wolves covered in sheep's clothing that are coming in the name of the Lord and devouring the foundation of our homes and nation. It is plain to see when we look through God's eye and His Word, that there are those who have been given over to a reprobate mind who will never change.

Someone told me the economy was doing great. I wonder where this person is getting information? Everything I have researched and see shows me that our banking system is a breath away from collapsing. I wonder if anyone realizes the impact that this will make on us and the world around us. Just that alone will be catastrophic! When you put that with corrupt politicians, the entitlement society, etc., it screams Marxism, and the death of true capitalism.

God has given us the inalienable right to choose between heaven and hell. I understand what the Christians are saying about Donald Trump and also understand the evil of Hillary. Laying that aside, I want to mention that it is plain for me to see and understand how Satan is preparing "we the people", through compromising to accept the anti-Christ establishment with the "One World Order". We are in the midst of that and many people don't see it. The Church is totally failing us! My warning is not to compromise your Godly principles and values to accept a lesser evil. Stay true to your Savior. Many people don't realize how the church has compromised itself through the 5013c. Through this tool to get money for the church, they have lost their moral compass and have watered down the Word to make it pleasing to people's ears and keep that money rolling in! "Cruise ship mentality"!

I have been contemplating over the years I have had Face Book, and I have observed that most people are not willing to change their life style. They try to fit Christianity into the life style they are accustomed to as opposed to what the Bible is really teaching the believer. What has made me notice this is the fluctuation of people who either "unfriend" me or else they are not willing to share. I think much of this is because many of them are too busy to be informed, they are caught up with the cares of this life, and it's out of fear of rejection from other people, who in turn are too progressive and liberal to sell themselves out to Christ and His teachings. I have observed this in the declining membership amongst the "uncompromised Word of God" church gatherings. This leads me to believe that they truly do not take the Word of God as the absolute truth and have no fear of His righteousness. My heart cries for those who compromise their salvation for the pathway of hell.

It is amazing how a City Council, or the Mayor, or the Governor of a state, can abuse the Bill of Rights and the Constitution with their power. We the people, who come in the name of the Lord, do nothing about it when we should be lodging complaints, and confronting them with the truth. Each one of us individually has the responsibility to be good stewards of God's Word. We must realize we will be accountable for that. You need to know that Sharia Law is coming to a city and state near you if we do not put a stop to it. You need to understand what Sharia Law is and how it opposes God's law. The state of Texas has already accepted Sharia law. This is the Bible belt we are talking about! If this can happen in Texas it's just a matter of time for "ungodly states," such as Washington State! Beware of Sanctuary cities as well, as these are those who oppose God's principles and values and uphold abominations sited in Romans: Chapter one of the Bible. We are ripe for the picking!

The eclipse

By the time you see this; the eclipse will have already passed. The world still exists! My concern or question is, I wonder how many people ignored everything they read or heard about needing special sun glasses and looked at the eclipse anyway with their naked eyes. If they did, they will pay the consequence for that sight. The Bible talks about looking to the heavens for signs of the times by looking at the alignment of the stars and planets. I am sure after September 23rd with the alignment of Virgo and the twelve stars surrounding the virgins head and the moon at her feet and Jupiter in her womb, we will be wondering, "was the Bible prophecy fulfilled"? It's my belief that God's Word always has been and always will be fulfilled. There is a reason why these signs, wonders, as well as parables and prophecies, that were written thousands of years ago, are being fulfilled. We all would be better off if we would heed to the teachings of the Creator. It's better to be ready for the rapture at all times than to find a date and time when it might happen and then get right with God. The rapture could happen before you get "right" with God!

I know there are many out there who have a lot of false information on the alignment of the planet and stars for the 23rd of September. With all the hoopla in the media about doomsday and the rapture, can't say I blame you! However the truth is that it does have significance for those who are the bride of Christ, "true believers", they know that it's a sign of preparing themselves for what is to come. There is a lot of Bible based information on this. It does point to Revelation. It is a biblical pivoting point in God's Word that should not be taken lightly. I have read a couple of books by Messianic Jews on this subject that was backed up excellently by scripture. Don't sell yourself short. Be praying for Israel and coming world events.

With all that is going on in the world these days, we must not lose sight of the fact that God can turn it into lemonade and bring serenity through it all. This is an opportunity to come to Christ and strengthen your relationship with Him. I have friends in Texas and Florida as well as in the areas of the west where there are major fires happening and yet there is still much hope for us all! <u>Jeremiah 10:13,</u> (NASB), "When He utters His voice, there is a tumult of waters in the heavens, And He causes the clouds to ascend from the end of the earth; He makes lightning for the rain, and brings out the wind from His storehouses".

God is in control! This is just the beginning of our times of tribulation and birth pains. It shall be as it was in the days of Noah. Then 120 years went by as People denied the truth as Noah spoke. You have heard about the volcano activity in Yellowstone and we have seen volcanoes and earthquakes; however we'll see them become even more active and violent. These are signs and the Lord is talking to us through these signs and should not be ignored.

Numbers 16:32, KJV, "And the earth opened her mouth, and swallowed them up, and their houses, and all the men that *appertained* unto Korah, and all *their* goods. This was because of their sinful ways and not obeying God's Word. They chose other gods to serve".

Zechariah 14:4, KJV, "And his feet shall stand in that day upon the mount of Olives, which *is* before Jerusalem on the east, and the mount of Olives shall cleave in the midst thereof toward the east and toward the west, *and there shall be* a very great valley; and half of the mountain shall remove toward the north, and half of it toward the south. It is easy to understand how this will affect us financially in the world market. It isn't just the United States that is bank-rupt but other nations so there would be your digital cashless society and the one world order.

Behavior response to executive orders and changes that President Trump is making is not surprising. In fact it tells me that there are always going to be those who never will choose principles and priorities over evil. What I find amazing however is that their actions are showing that they do not take the Word of God, the Constitution, and the Bill of Rights seriously. This shows in their childish and civil disobedient actions. The vast majority of people with this mentality do not want to learn or study the Word of God and the true heritage of our country. They are usually the entitlement class of people as well as liberals and progressives. They don't even realize that they are socialist well on their way to being communist or fascist. I want to point out that this proves the Bible to be correct once again and the prophecies that it tells us to watch for and warns us about.

The Lord has asked me to share this: Jeremiah 29:13, NASB, "And you will seek Me and find Me, when you search for Me with all your heart". This verse is primarily for the nation of Israel, but the principle is true for everyone. (Prov. 8:17; Ex. 33:13).

Mel's Psalm 10

O' beloved Master, Father of Abraham, Isaac, and Jacob: When all around me is grieving, and is in utter chaos and without hope how splendid I find it, that I can hide myself in thee! All the while singing praises unto you. And how I can prance and dance and feel your warm arms around me drawing me closer into your bosom. There I sense the honeysuckle and the smell of the lilies. And I rejoice for I know that I am saved from the tribulation that's coming bountiful upon the world. For it is not of you to bring this, but it's you that brings the righteousness and holiness and the light that I love to dance in. For you are my sight and you are my ears oh Heavenly Father let my tongue and my lips speak of your splendor and your love and the compassion that I would not have if it weren't for the righteousness of your words that dwell in me and melts my heart like honey. Written by Rev. Mel Jolley

Chapter Twenty-Five
Pulpit

We need to hear from our pulpits the vision and clear word that our founders knew to be true. Citizens today must become mindful of the "Divine" principle of national accountability. We should look at national policies proposed by our current political leaders and ask, "In light of the principle of national accountability, what will be the result of this proposed policy?" Certainly, there will be neither rewards nor punishments. But there are many policies that the Bible makes clear are of direct concern to God—the shedding of innocent blood by taking the lives of the unborn, the rejection of heterosexual marriage as God established it, prohibiting citizens from acknowledging God in public, the taking of private property by government, etc. To consider the inescapable spiritual effect of a political leader's public policy positions is not just a question of idle musing. Those positions can have a direct impact on the quality of life for every individual in a community, state, and nation. Evaluating Divine consequences for specific public policies is vital to the preservation of sound government and retaining God's blessings on the country.

A point of interest

We are studying the Book of Deuteronomy in a home Bible group. We are applying it to our current world and our country's situation. In doing this something came to my mind. In Duet 2:4-5, (KJV), "And command thou the people, saying, Ye are to pass through the coast of your brethren the children of Esau, which dwell in Seir; and they shall be afraid of you: take ye good <u>heed</u> unto yourselves therefore: [5] Meddle not with them; for I will not give you of their land, no, not so much as a foot breadth; because I have given mount Seir unto Esau for a possession".

Key word is <u>heed</u>. "Take ye good heed". Many of us don't understand what the meaning of heed is. Surely none of us want to hear a compromised word or experience the discipline of God's hand and His righteousness. It seems that we are fed an overload of compromising and God's love and mercy with no discipline. The lack of accountability will send us straight to hell. We as a nation have lost our moral compass and direction with God directly because we have turned our backs on the uncompromised word of God and have conformed to words of progressives and liberals. You can see the falling away of the church, when they no longer speak of political issues in the pulpit.

China

It is written, every nation works it's salvation through the Word of God. Every knee shall bow, every tongue confess that Jesus Christ is Lord. The head of China came to Seattle, Washington and visited our nation's capital. I love my Chinese brothers and sisters in the Lord; however our Pastors must speak the truth about evil from the pulpit so that we will learn that the truth is found in the Word of God. Pastors can't be worried about who is offended, the offended need to repent. We should be aware of the evil and deception that comes from China's leadership. They are into internet espionage with big business and our government. They no longer want to accept the American currency. They want a "One World Order". Those elected officials in our government from Olympia to Washington D.C. who embrace this evil are in bed with China, Islam, sexual immorality, and all aspects of evil. They must be aware of their destination which is hell if they continue to sleep with evil. Our spiritual leaders are just as guilty. This is something that didn't happen overnight.

Chapter Twenty-Six
Leviathan Spirit

Mel's Psalm #4

I can't keep from rejoicing in your awesome power and glory. Even when darkness falls all around me, and those brothers and sisters that cry out because they worry about their status and what may come to be. And I see tribulation that abounds all around us like ravening wolves and lions that are trying to rip us apart! But yet I can find exceeding happiness that never ceases to astound me, like a well of water that bubbles up from deep within that keeps refreshing me and I know this to be true that it flows from your throne. When your spirit touches my heart and I sing praises unto your name I know that I don't need to be ashamed just to let myself go and fly with your presence. I seem to soar like the eagles on high. I've never felt so much comfort from within and happiness since I found the secret, which isn't a secret, to come into your presence.

Written by Rev. Mel Jolley

I began speaking on the subject of the "Leviathan" spirit quite some time ago. It is squeezing the Holy Spirit out of the Church in America, as we know it. I would like to share scripture with you on "Leviathan". Within these scriptures you will see what Leviathan is, and how the scripture illustrates its behavior. America is consumed with this "Leviathan" spirit, as the church is today. It even affects those believers who do not stay steadfast in the Word of God. **Isaiah 27:1** (KJV), "In that day the LORD with his sore and great and strong sword shall punish leviathan the piercing serpent, even leviathan that crooked serpent; and he shall slay the dragon that is in the sea". When we are filled with the Holy Spirit, we speak as living waters that flow from within us. It's likened unto the river that flows from the throne of God. **Psalm 46:4 (KJV),** "4 there is a river, the streams whereof shall make glad the city of God, the holy place of the tabernacles of the "Most High". But the Leviathan spirit dwells underneath the waters and is willing to take down those who do not stay true to God's word, the Spirit of the Lord. We think of Job as being righteous. Indeed he was because he stood firm and steadfast in the righteousness of the Lord and defeated his battle over the Leviathan Spirit and was rewarded for the persecution and torment that he went through. Read Job 41 which gives you an accurate description of Leviathan.

Perhaps give thought to this. To keep it simple what is going on in the world is "Good" versus "evil". Denial is not good. I put that into the evil drawer because everything that is not good is evil. The Bible tells us God sends us forth as sheep in the midst of wolves: "be wise as serpents and harmless as doves". This means to be quick and alert in using His word. Fear is the beginning of wisdom. Proverbs 9:10,(ASV),"10 The fear of Jehovah is the beginning of wisdom; And the knowledge of the Holy One is understanding". I have spoken about the Leviathan spirit before, and it is taking over the church of today which causes mass confusion amongst the brethren and leaders of the church. Read 1 Corinthians 14:33, "For God is not a God of confusion but of peace".

Read 2 Timothy 2:7, "Think over what I say, for the Lord will give you understanding in everything." Believe me that there will be a day when the Messiah will come back and cleanse the church from its foolishness and wickedness. To those who want to go to a coffee house, go to a coffee house, but don't go to church for coffee. Likewise to those who are into strobe lighting and smoke shows and want to see cleavage and legs which is of the flesh and lustful, feel free to go to your favorite dance club or disco. We are not in church to hear what our itching ears want to hear. We are there to prove ourselves worthy of the knowledge and wisdom of God's word.

Matthew 21:13 (NAS), "And He said to them, "It is written, 'MY HOUSE SHALL BE CALLED A HOUSE OF PRAYER'; but you are making it a ROBBERS' DEN." The Church is guilty of robbing and twisting the Word of God which leads to confusion and not focusing on the Living Word. I hope we can see how this affects our whole lifestyle, the way we deal with legislation, and school boards as well as city Hall and our immediate families' values.

Yes we have heard about discipline. And to have discipline brings serenity and peace. Hebrews 12:11 (NKJV),"11 Now no chastening seems to be joyful for the present, but painful; nevertheless, afterward it yields the peaceable fruit of righteousness to those who have been trained by it".

Read Luke 6:27-36. Love your enemies, do good to those who hate you, bless those who curse you, pray for those who mistreat you. Turn the other cheek if slapped. If they take your coat, give them your shirt also. Give to everyone who asks, and if anyone takes your belongings, don't demand it back. Do to others as you would have done to you.

It is my belief in these matters that many of us have been deceived by Satan, or the Leviathan spirit, by not putting into action what we learn from Proverbs and James. We should be good stewards of God's word in all matters. We are not to be co-dependent, enabling people to continue in their way of sin. We have to rely on the Holy Spirit to guide us in all situations. God is not asking us to live a double standard or to be abused by the evil one. Use wisdom when applying the above scriptures to your life.

Please read Ephesians 1:4-23 in your Bible. We the people must not believe the lies of the Leviathan spirit. I am in agreement with President Trump and what he has shared about the NFL, not participating in the pledge of allegiance to the flag. Let it be known that this goes much deeper than just disrespecting the flag and national anthem. The lies of racial inequality coming from these high rollers in the corporate world of sports is just more poison from this den of vipers to destroy the very roots of this covenant nation that was founded on Christian- Judeo principles and values.

There is no credit in loving those who love you back.

Sinners do that. There is no credit in doing good to those who do good to you. Sinners do that. There is no credit in lending to others when you are going to be paid back. Sinners do that. Love and do good to your enemies and lend without expecting to get paid back. Your reward will be great. You will be a child of the Most High because He is kind to the wicked and ungrateful ones. Be merciful as your Father is merciful. In the matter of giving, God wants us to give. Do not lend unless you are willing to give. You cannot expect all to repay. This would be the heart of Christ to give, rather than lend. Lending can cause problems when the item lent out is not returned. Satan can use such a situation to cause problems in a friendship if one does not comply. Not everyone including, Christians, have the heart or mind of God.

Chapter Twenty-Seven
Agenda 21

The Lord has asked me to share this: "And you will seek Me and find Me, when you search for Me with all your heart", Jeremiah 29:13 (NKJV). This verse is primarily for the nation of Israel but the principle is true for everyone. Read (Prov. 8:17; and Ex. 33:13). Many of you probably don't know this dirty little secret of the government; it has to do with socialism and Marxism. I was born blind and had both eyes removed. I went to a state school for the deaf-blind and developmentally disabled in Washington State. Through the years progressively I have seen how socialism has attracted people of liberal mind and progressiveness. From the outside it looks good. But from the inside you are held in bondage and you are controlled by the government as well as limited by them. It is likened to a drug. I have worked in sheltered workshops that are designed by the government to help people of disabilities with the goal of making them independent. This was the beginning of Agenda 21. However, the truth is, it's just another way to control the masses. These programs of opportunity by the government are just another way to put people into bondage, by perpetuating jobs for the liberal and progressive minded

middle to upper class. Now we are to the point where
DSHS and the Obama-care programs along with Margaret
Sanger's frame of mind, can and are more than willing to
dispose of the unnecessary people who they choose. All of
these sheltered workshops pay a substandard slave wage. The
items that the people of disability need for their disability
are hugely inflated, such as tools that they need to perform
their jobs and life style. Government housing usually is
run down because these programs take self-respect out of
the equation and replace it with entitlement so there is no
need to maintain or care for their properties. This same
philosophy works with our growth and salvation with Jesus
Christ. When we don't actively seek the truth and display
the truth and destroy socialism and Marxism, we will end
up with slavery and tyranny for all. Evil would prevail then
and this is why we need the truth of God's Word.

To the followers of Jesus Christ we know it wouldn't
have made much difference if it was Hillary Clinton or
Trump in the Oval office. It is known that the "left" wants
a "global world order". For this reason, I stress that it is
important for us to know God's Word and to change our
life style to what our Heavenly Father desires for us. He is
the only one who can control our true destiny. As long as
the strongest nation in the world, the United States, keeps
rejecting God's principles and values, we will see a one world
order, a revolution, and continued tribulation and chaos.
This has been prophesied in the Bible and will come to pass.

For those who are interested, or have an inquiring mind,
this is about the youth who are protesting. You need to do
your research and find out who is supporting Common

Core and Agenda 21. Check out what these organizations are doing to brain wash the youth for a One World Order. This movement is a continuation of the movement which was happening in the 60's. You would be surprised who is involved with this! The same people who did this in the 60's are funding these organizations. Bill Ayers, George Soros, Van Jones and the Clintons. This is a continuation of what started in the 60's, which actually started in the early 1900's. Obama is a product of this. The goal is for a One World Order. I lived during this in the 60's, and here it is again! Beware of who Donald Trump is appointing. He has the Ultright, Britebart, and Steve Banning so far. See how these people are linked together.

We the People have allowed and encouraged the Anti-Christ and One World Order by supporting them through legislation and voting on resolutions for Agenda 21. If you know nothing about Agenda 21 you should seriously study up on it. Many things that we have passed thinking that it would be good for us have played right into their hands to take away freedom and activities and to hold you in bondage. For instance have you ever wondered about all these bike trails? Why are cities sponsoring bikes for the public to use? While all the time they are making cars so expensive to have and maintain by raising taxes on gas and license fees. I know where we live they do not charge a bicycle license fee to maintain and support bike trails and lanes. If you noticed, they are putting up an abnormal amount of condos and apartments in a compound fashion. They also have their hands in government lands and forestry. They are involved in your health care and wellbeing which includes care facilities such as nursing homes. It is a number one driver of euthanasia and abortion. I would encourage you to look into this more.

I am amongst those who find it quite disturbing when relatives and friends do not see the writing on the wall that "prophecy" has and is being fulfilled in our lifetime. It's all because of the dumbing down that has occurred in the last sixty to seventy years. Yes I know we can go further back than that. It looks like the Leviathan spirit, "Satan," has us right where he wants us, when Americans aren't willing to uphold the Word of God and their national documents. It seems that we have relinquished the education of our youth to an anti-Christ spirit and government because the people refuse to understand what progressiveness and liberalism have to do with entitlement programing. We are going to continue to see prophecy being fulfilled regardless of what the people choose to do because of this programing of one's mind and it just gets worse until they become reprobate. The Bride of Christ is like-minded people who have surrendered their lives over to Christ. They must rise up and prepare themselves for the coming battle. Praying for souls and watching people's lives change through Christ has to be the most important miracle in our lives. We must take the responsibility as children of the Lord to take back our destiny and freedom for our nation and for control of our families. We have been shown the way through the scripture. There lies your hope.

Common Core

Over the years the Republicans and Democrats have fragmented so much neither one stands for the values they once had. Both have entered into Communism and Marxism, which is dangerous to American freedom and values. A few years back many of you heard of the "Common Core" program for the public school systems. Its purpose was to brain wash the youth and does not give a true picture of American history. It was to lead them into believing socialism and progressiveness and political correctness could soothe the problems of today by just throwing money at the given situation, not realizing the effect it has on the economy and the market. The "Common Core" idea is still in effect but is now using different names. Local news media and "Common Core" in the school systems under other various descriptions, not always called Common Core, are other tools being used to shed our Christianity and Christian culture.

Years ago it would not have been difficult to teach people the difference between a conservative and a liberal, or to compare them to a socialist or a Marxist? The people forget nothing is free, and the entitlement society is selling our souls and making us slaves to the government. Bondage big time! This philosophy is causing the world market to crash which means we will have to go to a different currency and a One World Order. The youth of today does not know how all these things interconnect which causes total destruction and chaos. Too few people take the time to read and apply God's Word for the answers. The number one excuse is being too busy to read and apply God's Word.

CHAPTER TWENTY-EIGHT
Prophetic

We need to realize that we are accountable for who we elect to political office, as well as who we choose as spiritual leaders. For example, it is not of the Lord to make deals or compromise with Satan or the enemy. We are aware of those running for political office, but must become more aware of those in church leadership, who insist on compromising the word of God by giving their approval to ungodly candidates, and influencing their congregations to follow suit. As individuals we will be accountable!

This passage is often misunderstood. Christ Jesus is talking to a Covenant nation. Keep in mind that the only other covenant nation is America. This will help you to understand Ezekiel 38 and 39, and the events that we are going through at this time. In my opinion, we are now closing in on the zero hour, or we are actually in the zero hour. Read Ezekiel 38:10-15. The Lord said it will come about that thoughts will come into your mind and you will devise an evil plan and will say I will go up against the land of unprotected villages. I will go against those who are at rest and live securely, to capture spoil and plunder to turn your hand against the waste places which are now inhabited and against the people who are gathered from the nations who acquired cattle and goods, which live at the center of the world. Sheba, Dedan, and merchants of Tarshis will say have you come to capture spoil? Prophesy and say to Gog, on that day when my people Israel are living securely, will you not know it? You will come from your remote parts of the north, you and many people with you, riding horses, as a mighty army. Be aware of those who make deals. There is always compromise, deals. Do you want to deal with Russia, China, or Islam? Be steadfast in God's Word.

The Judgment

Read Matthew 25:31-40. When Jesus comes in His glory, with all the angels, He will sit on His throne. All nations will be gathered together before Him. He will separate them as a shepherd separates the sheep from the goats. The sheep will go on His right and the goats will go on His left. The King will say to those on His right, "you are blessed of my Father; inherit the kingdom prepared for you from the foundation of the world. I was hungry and you gave me something to eat. I was thirsty, and you gave me something to drink; I was a stranger and you invited me in, naked and you clothed me, sick, and you visited me, in prison and you came to me". Then the righteous will say "when did we see you as a stranger, or naked and cloth you, or sick or in prison and come to you?" The King will answer them, "to the extent that you did it to one of these my brothers, even the least of them, you did it to me." For the rest of the story finish reading Matthew 25.

There is more than one of you out there who feels

trapped "like in a prison" and there is no way out. That is a lie from Satan and there is a way out! There are many people in this world who are trapped in their own bodies even because of a serious accident, or mental, or medical condition. Then there are those imprisoned by their own foolish choice of rebellion. Yet there is another segment of people who may not even realize that they are held captive by their own self willingness not to improve their life styles and they think they are hiding behind a mask. Those remind me of Paul and Silas in the book of Acts, chapter 16. The Lord is speaking to you; He sees a broken, sincere heart. He has a special inner healing for you even while you are reading this and the spirit of the Lord is going to set your spirit free like a lonely lost dove. You will be healed physically or emotionally from this day forth you will have the hunger for His food and the feast He has for you. Praise God He came to set the captives free!

Speaking for myself I have felt after Obama, "the son of perdition", vacates the white House he will go to work for the United Nations. He will continue his work toward a One World Order which will work hand in glove with the man- child, Donald Trump, who took over the oval office. Donald Trump will not realize that he is being used as a pawn. He is the man everyone was clamoring for. Big business and a big mouth know how to excite the people for what they want their itching ears to hear. He also knows how to compromise the Word of God to make it acceptable. Putin has been setting himself up to take over the oil in OPEC. We are continuing to see the actual gross evil being poured out through the nations. It will continue to get worse. Many of us have heard this for decades now, but if you stop and watch it in real time it's easy to see how rapidly these things are coming to pass.

When it comes to the Book of Revelation and "End time prophecy", I have found most people are seeking information that is not in scripture; or they want to know the precise date and time of the return of Christ. None of us will find this there. The Bible clearly says no man knows the day or hour. Matthew 24:36, KJV, "But of that day and hour knoweth no *man*, no, not the angels of heaven, but my Father only". Think of the book of Revelation as any other book of the Bible. Back it up with previous books of scripture. The book of Revelation clearly gives us road signs to watch for. You would find some in Matthew, as well as the other Gospels, Deuteronomy, Ezekiel, Daniel, and Isaiah for instance.

Read 1Timothy 4:1. In the latter times some shall depart from the faith, giving into seducing spirits, and doctrines of devils. Read Hebrews 6:4-6. It is impossible for those who were once enlightened and had a heavenly gift, the Holy Spirit, and knew the Word of God and the powers of the world to come; that if they fall away, to renew them again to repentance, because that would crucify the Son of God once again and put Him to open shame.

Read Revelation 2:4-5. You have lost and left your first love. Remember from where you fell and repent and do the first works, or else I will come unto you quickly and will remove your candlestick out of His place, except you repent! It is possible to lose your salvation! Read 2 Corinthians 11:3. As the serpent deceived Eve through his subtlety, so your minds could be corrupted from the simplicity of Christ.

As you can see from these scriptures, we are in the "falling away" of the church and are living this right now!

We must understand what the bride and the groom is, regarding the ten virgins in Matthew. The Lord is speaking about the church. He is the "Groom" and the church is the "Bride". It does not have anything to do with denominations or a particular label. One of the main purposes of the Book of Revelation is to impress upon us as individuals to be sensitive to the warnings and road signs that God has given to prepare us for His coming. It is not necessary to know the exact day or time, as we have been told.

Spiritual dream

For those who believe in spiritual dreams, I have them sometimes and will share one with you. In my dream I was asked to speak at a large gathering of people. There was TV media there. I wasn't actually prepared, but I knew the Holy Spirit wanted me to speak. For me, that is normal. When I was being helped to the front, and directed to face the people, there was a disturbance that caused the cameras to react and the media became worried. Someone came over and touched me and said "everything would be ok, just start when you are ready". That person who touched me introduced me and had me turn my back towards the group of people. On my jacket it said "Branded" and there was a Star of David with a cross inside of the star. I spoke, that you don't need to fear if you are following Christ's principles and values. Do not be ashamed to stand for Jesus Christ. The time is coming when the Spirit of the Lord will come upon you and you will be tested. You will know if your life is threatened because out of your mouth your words will become fire and they will evaporate that person threatening you. That same power will be given unto you and you will meet the need to protect those who have chosen to follow Jesus Christ. I am sharing this because this dream was extremely real and it goes with a vision that God gave me years ago. In the vision I was told there will be a time when I will be standing before a large group of people, and I will physically see Jesus. I also own two jackets with "Branded "on the back of them. They both have a Star of David with a cross in the middle of the star. You remember that the Bible referred to three crosses. Jesus was in the middle. On His right side, the thief saw that He was Jesus and asked for forgiveness of his sins. Jesus told him "this very night you will be in paradise with me". I am sharing this, to encourage you, to be prepared for what is coming soon.

Does this scripture apply to today, and if so, where at?

Read 2nd Timothy 3:1-7. In the last days perilous times will come. Men will be lovers of themselves, lovers of money, boasters, proud, blasphemers, disobedient to parents, unthankful, unholy, unloving, unforgiving slanderers, without self-control, brutal, despisers of good, traitors, headstrong, haughty, lovers of pleasure rather than lovers of God, having a form of godliness but denying its power. Turn away from such people! For of this sort are they who make captives of gullible women full of sin, led away through lust, always learning and never able to come to the knowledge of the truth. If you uphold to this exhortation you will not be "politically correct", but you will be "righteously right".

Read 2nd Timothy 4:1-5. Jesus Christ will judge the living and the dead at His appearing and His Kingdom. I charge you to preach the Word, be ready in and out of season. Convince, rebuke, exhort, with longsuffering and teaching. The time will come when men will not endure sound doctrine, but according to their own desires, they will heap up for themselves teachers and will turn their ears away from the truth and believe fables. Be watchful in all things, endure afflictions, do the work of an evangelist, fulfill your ministry.

I am not a defeatist or a "gloom and doom" person, but I know there are people who would beg to differ with me! However the Word of God, as well as history, proves that what I am saying is true. I come from the point of view that history, and the Word of God are the truth. I cannot give anybody a time table or appointed time when these things will come into play and increase, but rest assured they will be happening as calamity and dissention increases. We will start to see the suicide rate greatly sky rocket to unreal numbers. This has to do a lot with the price of medicine, groceries, and the world economy with banks and market crashes. The people will not know where to turn because of insurance issues and taxation without representation. I know people don't like to hear this; however we will see increases in forest fires, floods, tropical storms, earthquakes; and chaos and violence in our streets. If one would take the time to see how much these things have increased already, they should become aware in the past twenty years they are about to double and triple! This is caused because of "SIN", and the apostate church not repenting. We are actually fortunate to be living in these times to see the "hand of God" moving on our nation and the world!

For those who understand about the bear from the North and have studied end time prophecy, we truly don't know how long it takes prophecy to be fulfilled from beginning to end; it's all in God's time. Scripture is very clear on what will be happening. Obama and Putin have America and the USSR on the fast track to a One World Order. As we watch Syria and Jordan on one front, as well as North Korea on the second front, we definitely know that China is more than willing to side in with Russia. In saying this, I am not laying the blame all on Obama, but he is the one who put us on a fast track. Obama continues to seek his goals with the major news networks and in partnership; they are fueling the fire leading us to the end times!

I highly recommend the movie, "Return to the Hiding Place." It has a lot of insight for us Christians to apply to our lives especially for the end times.

We have come to a time when few are willing to renew their life style to a total commitment for Christ. Those who do will be mocked and persecuted for that choice. Too many are willing to take the easy road and the broad path to pleasure as we continue our journey to entitlements and silencing the freedom of speech for the believer! Our nation is going the way of the world, which is not God's way. The best thing that we can do is to pray for one another and ask God to open our minds.

Many of you have heard me speak about the "fallen Church". I would think that one could see the prophecy of the Lord fulfilled here. When you're able to distinguish the person who has a relationship with Christ, this is His glory! It's not an individual's glory, or the collected glory of a denomination, or religious organization or group. The scripture teaches that the true church is "The bride who does the will of The Father and lives by every Word that proceeds out of the mouth of God". (Matthew 4:4). With that in mind, I want to share this Promise that the Lord gave me to write some time ago for the church.

The Promise

Be ye still and walk in the presence of the Lord where you will not weary or grow faint. Know that you are the temple of the Lord where the lamp- stand shines as a path unto your feet. I am Omni present with you for you have the protection of my spirit that travels with you. You are covered by the shed blood of the Lamb that was slain for your ransom. As you drink from my cup, you shall have the peace and the knowledge as well as the serenity that was spoken in my Word. For you do know that I created all things and knew you before you were. For surely there will be days that you will want to grow faint and lay down, but I have told you that I am your strength and I am your righteousness and the glory is bestowed upon Me and your crown will be cast before the feet of Jesus, for you have not rejected, but have received Him. I have made you a place at the bridal feast where you have come prepared with the wedding garment. You were patient and strong, you thought you sat in the back, but I came and brought you to the forefront. Patiently you have waited, in the stillness you have felt my love, and my arms that surround you, and they more than comfort and soothe your heart and brought you into the true peace and serenity of my heart, because you are my child, not that of the world.

Written by Rev. Mel Jolley

CHAPTER TWENTY-NINE
Anti-Christ

My Father's Hand

As I hold onto my Father's hand, it seems so big to me. As my fingers reach across the breadth of His hand, it feels so strong and tough. I can feel the warmth coming from Him that feels like love and comfort. As we are walking I notice the sky starts to turn cloudy and gray. I realize without Him even speaking I know I am being protected and comforted, even while the clouds grow really dark and everything around me grows so loud with yelling and screaming and sirens blowing so many loud noises, coming all at once. I grow frightful and as my hand starts to slip I notice a deep scar on His hand and I hear His gentle voice say, "Don't you trust in me, your Father? You are my son you know. Just hold on to Me and I'll stand with you and beside you. We'll go through these trials and tribulations together". As we walk on it starts getting lighter and the clouds start moving away. The assurance from His hand begins to take over once again and I realize this is what blessed assurance means that I have more than just a Father or friend in Jesus Christ.

Written by Rev. Mel Jolley

To the angel of the Church in Laodicea:

Read Revelation 3:14-22. It says to write to the angel of the Church in Laodicea: These are from the ruler of God's creation. I know your deeds; you are not "hot or cold". I would prefer you to be either hot or cold. You are "luke" warm and I will spit you out of my mouth! You say because you are rich you don't need anything, but you don't realize how wretched, pitiful, poor, blind and naked you really are! Buy gold refined in the fire so you can be rich and wear white clothes to cover your shame and nakedness. Put salve in your eyes so you can see. I rebuke and discipline those whom I love. Earnestly repent! "I stand at the door and knock. Hear my voice and open the door and I will come in and eat with you, and you will see me. If you are victorious I will let you sit with me on my throne, just as I was victorious and sat with my Father on His throne. Whoever hears let them obey the Spirit and what it says to the Churches.

Is the beast here?

http://www.av1611.org/666/www_666.html Look this up on your computer.

666 in Hebrew is www. As we learn in studying the Bible, prophecies are fulfilled over a period of time. God is in control of that time. My opinion is that Obama is representing the son of perdition and the possibility is that Donald Trump could be the man- child. I say this because of the way things are lining up. Let's take a look at WWW. Or World Wide Web for example, in Hebrew it means

666, which in the Bible, and refers to the mark of the beast. I am finding this very interesting because Ray Kurtzwell from google is working with Silicon Valley on artificial intelligence, to help develop a digital society that will allow total control over our lives. It's obvious because of what is happening here in America, and Stockholm Sweden they are doing away with check-out counters in stores, keys, credit cards, security passes, and medical cards for insurance, pass words and so on, all in the name of convenience! You won't have to worry about stolen identity because the one world order will own your identity. All of this will be for "our convenience".

To those who are willing to accept it, the new buzz word will be Faith. I am asking you to receive as much understanding and knowledge of His Word as you can. There are many of you who are being prepared to step out in the usage and fullness of this word. You are being prepared and it will happen over an extended period of time. You will become more comfortable in dealing with the public, and people of your community. You know it's for the hard times that we are going to be facing. You have been chosen to do supernatural things. You will be speaking words of wisdom that you may not even see come to pass, but they will have a mighty impact on those you speak to. I am sharing this with you because this is outside of your denominational building churches. This will be in the open for all who will see.

Faith

I have had many people ask me what hope do we have, if these truly are the last days? For those who believe that we are in the end times, faith becomes very crucial. Many of us become predisposed and have so many worries, for instance, the mark of the beast and the coming digital cashless society. We worry about our health care and insurance. How are we to provide for ourselves and loved ones? I am a firm believer in the scriptures teaching us that these are the days that we will have to truly understand and rely on faith. Hebrews chapter 11 in the Bible is known as "The Hall of Faith". Perhaps that is because Hebrews 11:1 is the best place to find the Biblical definition of faith *"Now faith is the substance of things hoped for, the evidence of things not seen" (KJV)*. It is also the book and chapter that we can review for those heroes of faith, such as Abraham, Isaac, Jacob and others. The Bible uses the words faith and belief or believe interchangeably. Eternal life is received by grace through faith. Faith is the victory that overcomes the world and without <u>faith</u> it is impossible to please God (1 John 5:4; Hebrews 11:6).

Read Acts 11:22-24. The report of this came to the church in Jerusalem, and they sent Barnabas to Antioch. When he saw the grace of God, he was glad, and he exhorted them all to remain faithful to the Lord and be steadfast in purpose. He was a good man, full of the Holy Spirit and faith and because of this; many people were added to the Lord.

Read these scriptures:

1 Corinthians 16:13. Watch, be firm in faith and be strong.

2 Corinthians 5:6-7. Always be of good courage. While we are in the body we are away from the Lord. We walk by faith, not sight. **By faith I believe the Word of God to be the absolute truth.** He has said I will supply all your needs.

Philippians 4:19. God will meet all your needs.

Read Matthew 14:13-21. We will have to have a behavior life changing experience in order for this kind of miracle to happen. As you can see this only applies to the true believer.

Remember when President John Kennedy was assassinated how the whole world was shocked? Some said it was the "bullet heard around the world" because it was known instantly. There is no nation or country that hasn't heard the Gospel. Thanks to the computer that has brought us the Bible instantaneously! It takes the Gospel everywhere! Through the computer I can understand how the whole world can see in real time the coming of the Messiah, for Christians the second coming!

Read Matthew 24:3-14. The Disciples asked Him when will this happen and what will be the sign of your coming and the end of the world? Jesus told them not to be deceived. Many would claim to be Him, deceiving even the believers. There will be rumors of wars, but it won't mean the end is here yet! Nation will rise against nation, kingdom against kingdom. Famines and earthquakes will happen in various places. This is only the beginning! You will be persecuted and put to death; you will be hated by all nations because they hate Jesus. Many will turn away from the faith and betray and hate each other. Many false prophets will appear and deceive many. Love will grow cold and wickedness will increase. Stand to the end to be saved. The gospel will be preached in the whole world as a testimony to all nations, and then the end will happen.

Face Book Letter

There are good spirits and bad spirits. Please do not become discouraged or depressed. I was asked how one knows if we are in a great awakening. The answer would be, "by the fruit". People are at different levels in their spiritual walk with God. How do you know if you are born again or saved? How does one know if they are spirit filled or not? There will be many people who will not be caught up in the great awakening, those being the spiritual dead people. This awakening was not intended to be in the church as we know it, it's outside the church because the church is corrupt, rejecting God's Word and His truth and principles which are specifically for the "bride" or body of Christ. They are the ones who are servers and workers. One might say "the army of Gideon". By observing with the spirit of God, and discerning what is happening in America and the world, you can see the hand of God moving. Remember in Birmingham, Alabama on August 28th, 2015, thirty-thousand people showed up who were seeking the truth and God's principles and values.

Out of fifty people speaking outside the capital, Washington D.C., Wednesday, September 9, 2015, I dare say there were four of them who gave a message of real significance. We must remember this is a spiritual battle we are fighting between good and evil, and not to please man. Very few people will actually be caught up in the awakening. The rest will be left behind out of ignorance and stubbornness. Saturday, September 12th, 2015, in Orlando Florida, there will be people meeting with the same principles and values. It's called the 9/12 summit. What this event is doing is telling the world and America to be prepared for the coming of the Messiah. The real question is, are we prepared for Jesus return? I am waiting to see a movement happen in Washington State.

Daniel, chapter 8

As I was reading in the book of Daniel, chapter 8, it talked about the horns of the ram and goat. The goat had one notable horn and the ram had two horns. The goat rushed at the ram and broke his two horns and the goat's horn also broke. The goat was the victor and from his broken horn four smaller horns appeared. Gabriel explained the meaning of the vision that Daniel had in Chapter 8, starting with Daniel 8:17. He came near where I was standing and I became frightened and fell on my face. He said to me "understand, son of man, for the vision is for the end of time. I fell into a deep sleep, but he touched me, and I, set upright. He said, "I will make you know what shall be in the end time of the indignation; for it's for the appointed time of the end. The ram, with the two horns, are the king of Media and Persia. The rough he-goat is the King of Greece; and the great horn between his eyes is the first King. And for that which was broken in place of where four stood up, four kingdoms will stand up out of the nation, but they won't have power. And in the latter time of their kingdom, the transgressors will come to the full and a fierce King knowing evil will stand up. He will have mighty power which is not his own, and shall destroy and prosper and do his pleasure, and he will destroy all the mighty ones and Holy people. Through his policy, craft will prosper, he will magnify himself, and security will be destroyed for many. He will stand up against the prince of princes; but he will be broken. The visions told are true, but the visions were shut up for the future. Reading about this got me to thinking about Revelation, where it talks about the ten horns and ten nations. The end times are very significant to us believers, and the Lord wants us to understand the messages He has given us in Daniel and Revelation. The Lord talked about this period of time in Daniel, and then again in Revelation, through John the "Beloved".

Read Revelation, Chapter 17. "The angel said to me, why are you astonished? The secret meaning of the woman and the beast, with the seven heads and the ten horns, that carries her, I will reveal to you. The beast that you saw was, and is not, and is about to come up from the abyss and go to destruction. Those who live on the earth whose names have not been written in the book of life from the foundation of the world will be astonished when they see the beast that was, and is not, and will be present again. Seven heads are seven mountains on which the woman is seated. There are seven kings, five have fallen, one is, the other has not yet come, and when he comes, he must remain for a little while. The beast that was and is not, is himself an eighth king; yet belongs to the seven and is going to destruction. The ten horns you saw are ten kings who have not yet received a kingdom, but will receive authority as kings with the beast for one hour. Their one purpose is to give their power and authority to the beast. These will make war against the Lamb, but the lamb, Jesus Christ will conquer them because He is Lord of lords and King of kings. Those with Him are called, chosen, and faithful."

We must pay attention to what is happening in today's news including the world news. If you have noticed, we have been put on a fast track since 2009. Nations have been failing and power has been changing. It is critical that we watch which nations these have been. Some names have even changed. Since 2009, the leadership of America has prompted these acts.

Read Revelation, chapter 13. The prophet saw a beast coming out of the sea. He had ten horns and seven heads. His horns were ten diadems, and on his heads were blasphemous names. The beast was like a leopard, his feet were like bear's, and his mouth was like a lion's mouth. The dragon gave him power, his throne, and authority. One of his heads appeared to be fatally wounded, but the fatal wound was healed. The whole earth was amazed and followed the beast. The dragon was worshipped because he gave authority to the beast. They worshipped the beast, saying who is like the beast? Who can wage war against him? A mouth was given to him to speak boasts and blasphemies. He was given authority to act for forty-two months. He spoke blasphemies against God; he blasphemed God's name and dwelling, and those who dwell in heaven. He was permitted to war against the saints and conquer them. He was given authority over every tribe, people, language, and nation. All who live on the earth will worship him; everyone whose name was not written from the foundation of the world in the Book of Life of the Lamb was slaughtered. You better pay attention. If anyone is destined for captivity, into captivity he goes. If anyone is to be killed with a sword, with a sword he will be killed. This demands perseverance and faith from the saints.

This should give us plenty of thought on how much America has played into the hands of evil. As we sit and watch, it continues to develop before our eyes! Who has actively been destroying the constitution of a covenant nation of God? Who in our elective government has been aiding and abetting the United Nations and our enemies who want to destroy America and Israel?

Read 2Thesalonians 2:3-13. Apostasy comes first, and then the man of lawlessness is revealed. The son of destruction opposes and exalts himself above every god or object of worship. Then he takes his seat in the temple of God, proclaiming himself as being God. Don't be deceived; don't forget that you were warned about this when Jesus was with you! You know what restrains him, but in His time, he will be revealed. The Lord will slay him with the breath of His mouth and bring the end at the appearance of His coming. God will send upon the unbelievers a deluding influence so that they will believe lies and will be judged who did not believe the truth and took pleasure in wickedness.

Many question about the Anti-Christ. Read 1John, 2nd John, and 3John, in your Bible. You will get the truth from the Word and not of man. In applying the Word, I'd like to illustrate something to you about this. Take a look at Hillary Clinton, and Donald Trump; and for those who live in the

State of Washington, Patty Murray, Maria Cantwell, and Jay Inslee; we can see by scripture who they serve.

We can see what the Anti-Christ is and the truth is. Look at Jude, only 1 chapter, 1:3-4 (NIV). Jude wrote, "I was eager to write to you about the salvation we share, but I am compelled to urge you to contend for the faith that was entrusted to God's holy people. Certain people whose condemnation was written about secretly slipped in among you. They are ungodly and pervert the grace of God to give license for immorality and deny Jesus Christ as the only sovereign Lord". We cannot "legislate" sin into law. This is why we need to know what is going on around us starting with our own neighborhood. We need to see how it affects our cities, counties and nation.

The book of Revelation is not that difficult to understand when we have the knowledge of the Old Testament and a clear vision of the tabernacle. For instance, do you know what the lamp stand signifies? With this knowledge and wisdom, I can now see with the Holy Spirit, Ezekiel 38 and 39 here in this passage of Revelation 2:9-11. We are told that the Lord knows our works, tribulation, and poverty, and we are rich! He knows the blasphemy of those who say they are Jews, who are not. Don't fear the persecution that you are about to suffer. The devil is going to throw some into prison, to be arrested and you will have tribulation. Remain faithful until death, and you will have the crown of life. Listen to what the Spirit is saying to the churches and obey! If you overcome you will not be hurt by the second death. It is easy to understand a covenant nation such as the U.S.A., as the little lion or the eagle, which clearly gives me the feeling that something mighty is going to start to happen soon.

We as Christians need to realize that there is a serious problem amongst the people who call themselves believers in the "Church". It is we the people who have to realize that there is a brood of vipers that have no regard for God's principles and values that has made its way into the government, which is full of officials, which we have voted into office. This has happened because the Leviathan spirit has squeezed the life out of the church.

What does the Bible say about vipers? Matthew 23:33, (NIV), "You snakes! You brood of vipers! How will you escape being condemned to hell"? Until the real believer who is the Bride of Christ stands up for the moral values and principles of God we will continue to be asked to vote for the lesser of two evils, one might call Beelzebub and Satan. I will not be part of those who vote between two evils. I find it interesting that there were 17 republican candidates to begin with and out of that number God gave us several choices with integrity, principles, and values. One might even say a love for our Heavenly Fathers' Word, yet this is what we were asked to choose from? Trump or Hillary!

Think about this. Well over 2000 years ago Jesus died, and people have been telling His story ever since. For me as a believer, these difficult times are not scary; however they do not please, or make me happy either. It grieves my soul that we have given away all our liberties and freedoms that the Word of God has given us. We have allowed snakes to come into all branches of our judiciary and governmental offices. It amazes me how the Word of God has warned us about vipers. It was a serpent that came to Eve in the garden, if you remember. Also a serpent visited the Son of God, Jesus, and tempted Him. It was also a viper that bit the apostle Paul when he was washed ashore from ship wreck and was building a fire. Everyone was amazed when Paul did not die. It was a sign that he was a murderer and when he did not die, they believed the sign revealed that Paul was a "god" instead. Paul quickly reassured them that he was only a man like themselves. This shows us that integrity, principles and values are worthy of being committed to, and standing up for. In Matthew 12:34, NIV, Jesus said: [34] "You brood of vipers, how can you who are evil say anything good? For the mouth speaks what the heart is full of".

We have come to the time "top down, bottom up and there is no trust amongst men. "As individuals we need to come to the place where we are totally sold out to the Word of God, the "Truth". Put God's Word first in all things, for God's rights, are for all. Stop thinking about self, and equal rights. Focus on the Creator of all things!

True and False Disciples

Matthew 7:21 (NIV), [21] "Not everyone who says to me, 'Lord, Lord,' will enter the kingdom of heaven, but only the one who does the will of my Father who is in heaven".

STOP! You cannot reason logically with Satan and the anti-Christ mentality. It happens to be that the majority of the people who want to change the Constitution do not understand God's principles and values. Therefore people will get what they want, an "entitlement society", which will not please them; and a "nanny" One World Government which will not please them. All just because they are too blind and stiff necked to understand that God's principles and values are for all and they can have what they want in Christ. Christ is the very one who they reject!

We as brothers and sisters in the Lord better wake up to the fact that things are much worse than what we really realize. It is more important to understand our Jewish foundation, heritage, and covenant with Christ. Stay informed about the things that are taking place right now with the bear from the north, "Russia", Putin, and Dugan. If you don't know anything about Dugan I would advise you to study up on who Alexander Dugan is. He is from Russia and probably is one of the scariest of the three top men in the world. He supports Donald Trump and has the same philosophy as Isis. This man influences most of the top men of the world including the military. See what great effects his cronies have on America and those who are in office and running for office along with the inner connection with Issis and George Soros. I suspect very soon there will be a major move by Russia.

There are many who think we are just at war with the Islam terrorist. I would like you to think with an open mind to connect the dots and allow the Holy Spirit to show you it's much greater than that. All of these have a common denominator: Progressives, Liberals, Socialist, Marxist, Communist, ACLU, Black Lives Matter, unions, and special interest groups. One must ask themselves if they have come to a place in their life where they realize that all of the above are anti-Christ. They do not uphold the principles and values of His living word. They meet the gratification

of the demented evil minded control freaks. They all hold
you in bondage, slavery, and take away your freedom that
God has provided you with in His Word.

We need to learn not to be angry, or have hatred towards
each other. We have to come to realize that we are fighting a
battle of principalities, good and evil. Understanding this is
to have the knowledge that anything that isn't of God is evil.
Therefore it comes from Satan, who is the evil one; thus the
battle of anti-Christ throughout this world. I have spent a
lot of time and effort on my Face Book and You Tube sight,
trying to teach that they are a "mindset". We must accept the
fact! One may want to look at their own state; I live in WA
State, which happens to be very anti-Christ. You can tell by
the fruit our state has, we have become one of the leading
states of the anti-Christ movements. We are the home of
CAIR, which is anti-Christ and promotes terrorism, foreign
gods, such as Allah, and Sharia Law. We are a state that
has a sanctuary city, Seattle, as well as others who want to
become sanctuary cities. We are a state that has embraced
homosexuality, same sex marriage, and unisex, non-gender
bathrooms, as well as leadership in the murdering of unborn
children, abortion, which is actually an act of worship to
Moloch, an ancient god. If this isn't enough, we also teach
our students' K-12, how to embrace it as the norm. By the
standard of anti-Christ, it's perfectly obvious we are now
living in the end times.

Read 2 Timothy 2:15. Study the scriptures to be
approved by God, a servant that will not be ashamed, rightly
dividing the word of truth. With this in mind, it's easy to
see who serves and follows the anti-Christ lifestyle, and who

chooses to live by God's Word. This battle will continue to rage with each and every one of us until Christ comes back.

Ok, I am going to give a passage from the Bible to verify. As we look at the news we are bombarded by the immorality, that we accept as "normal." We expose our children to immoral, unclean, corruption on TV, and the media daily, yet fail to see the corruption going on in our three branches of government. "It's no wonder we are going to hell in a handbasket"! Please read 2 Thessalonians 2:1-12 (NIV).

The Man of Lawlessness

We are told by the Disciples not to become unsettled or alarmed by the "teaching that the Lord already came back". Don't be deceived for the day will not come until the rebellion occurs and the anti-Christ is revealed. He will oppose and exalt himself over everything that is called "God or is worshipped". He sets himself up in God's temple proclaiming himself to be God! Don't you remember that God warned us about this? You know that He is holding the evil one back so that he may be revealed at the proper time. The secret power of lawlessness is at work, but the One who now holds it back will continue to do so, till he is taken out of the way. Then the anti-Christ will be revealed whom Jesus will over throw with the breath of His mouth and destroy by His coming. The anti-Christ will be in accordance with how Satan works. He will use all displays of power through signs and wonders that serve the lie. He will use all the ways of wickedness to deceive those who are perishing. They perish because they refused to love the truth and be saved. God sends them a powerful delusion so that they will believe the lie and be condemned.

For years I've been saying that if we want to know what's happening in America all we have to do is watch Israel where God's Word is being fulfilled. Individually it is up to us to seek the truth and have the willingness to allow the scripture to speak. A friend gave me a DVD, about the final battle of Armageddon, which is "Prophecy Revealed". I highly recommend that you watch and share this. Also watch The "Final Prophecies" DVD. I recommend "IN Our Hands", endorsed by CBN.com and the 700 club. Within the DVD's, take notes and you will see how the prophecy that the God of Abraham, Isaac and Jacob is being fulfilled. You will want your Bible with you, so you can back it up. This takes you from the Old Testament to the present time; and you will be able to identify the deceit of people, such as Jerimiah Right, Jessie Jackson, Rick Warren, and Joel Olsteen along with the government who are liberals and progressives, whom Satan is using.

There are many vipers out there determined to win Christians over to their cause. They will have charisma that will sway you to follow them blindly yet belittle you if you try to do your research. Putin, even now, is trying to sway those people who are not totally committed to the Lord. Rest assured he is not alone! Many of them are here in the United States. Van Jones is still very active, as well as the Clintons, George Soros and Bill Ayers and many others that Obama has appointed. There are too many to list here. They are all working for the same results. The ends justify the means. They do know that most people will not do their homework and that they have short memories and attention spans. They don't have the desire to connect the dots. That is why they have destroyed the educational school system, as well as the D.O.J., executive branch, and legislative branch of the government. The Declaration of Independence and the Bill of Rights have been compromised and no longer have meaning <u>because</u> they have been compromised. The News media just keeps filling us with poison and lies.

Anti-Christ

Many would argue the point about the "beast". However through studying the Bible and watching the history of Israel and the United States, It's easy to see how Satan has fulfilled prophecy by using the beast system. This has a direct effect on the world economy market as well. Ray Kurzweil and google with IBM and others have been networking together for artificial intelligence. It started out with credit cards, debit cards, rapidly changing to the point where there are many "cashless" stores and places of market. Digital currency is just a use of one's smart tech devices, which are the way of the future! If you have noticed this same technology is used in hospitals and medical centers with the wrist band and scanning. All smart technology interacts through private companies with the cooperation of the government and the One World Organization. This beast is well grounded in the world as well as our nation and was foretold thousands of years ago. A perfect example is "Sophie", a citizen, and most popular woman in Saudi Arabia. Sophie is a robot of "artificial intelligence", which is being perfected more and more every day to meet your needs. They have this in

Japan as well. Other nations including America are working on the same goal. For your general information there is an "AI church", which has been started already. Anthony Levandowski has created its first church.

The new religion of artificial intelligence is called "Way of the Future". This will rapidly grow as the most disguised "Christian Church" because of the compatibility that it will have for your desires and needs. It doesn't take too much of an imagination to see how this goes "hand and glove" with Common Core and Agenda 21 programs. Their philosophy is to keep the people 'simple and stupid educated idiots'. Their desire is to prevent you from understanding that God created that "gray matter" called the brain. It allows one to have the freedom of choice. Therefore the Anti-Christ is trying to extinguish the light of God, liberty, and freedom. You can see by this method how people have allowed themselves to become sluggards. Proverbs says they will no longer have the desire to think individually or study and listen to the Word of God. They will trade freedom for simplicity, and compromise their salvation, and exchange the lie for the truth!

Mel's Psalm 8

I come before you Father, seeking you through the tears of my heart. What do I behold? Yes that I see you upon that great steed, in all of your glory coming down out of the heavens. My ears even hear the pounding hooves and the Angels crying out for your glory. The leaves of the trees are clapping, and above all, the rocks are shouting "hosanna to the highest"! Even they know that you are the Master and the King of all. Here you come with peace and serenity abundantly. Here you come to protect those of your own. So long have they hungered and grown weak and tired, but there you are to reign once again in Jerusalem, from your holy temple, and your throne, to bring that sweet essence of your love. I find myself waiting for the doors of heaven to open up so that we would have your fullness. This is why those who call me brother will find me crying out in anguish, yes in anguish, for I know that you never intended to leave anyone behind. I want to be consumed by your passion!

Written by Rev. Mel Jolley

Chapter Thirty
Current Events

As you can see, nations also face the consequences for sin! God does not need our help or interference to make His promises or prophecies come true! This leads to our breaking covenant with Him. Not only we individually, but we as a nation!

I believe that we should be concerned about all of the evil, wicked, and foul people who Obama has pardoned and unleashed to the world. He was the President who has unleashed and pardoned viler, wicked prisoners, than any other President. If you do not know about these prisoners, you should do your homework and see the threat that they are bringing to America and the world. This is something you will not see in your news. It's similar to a door from hell being opened and demons released.

Our news media is corrupt.

I couldn't believe it when I saw CBS news showing a clip of an out of control, raging person, carrying on over Donald Trump. Calling America a democracy and having a fit because Donald Trump won the election! America was created as a republic! Many mistakenly call it a democracy.

Marjory Stoneman Douglas High School in Parkland, Florida

With regard to the shooting at Marjory Stoneman Douglas High School in Parkland, Florida: I do not believe that we need to lay any blame on President Trump. The blame goes to the congress and state senators. This is not a second amendment issue. However I do believe that this is a state government issue and not a federal government issue. The School boards need to decide to step up to the plate with their local government agencies and decide if they need similar security to the airports. This should come out of local tax dollars and not federal. Mental health issues are also local and not federal issues and should be recognized by teachers, counselors, school nurses and parents. If parents would be parents, things like this would not happen. We need to stop being co- dependent with the system and take on personal responsibility. We are not a police state yet.

CNN's debate on Wednesday Feb 21, 2018 about firearms in school and school shootings: The audience was loaded with supporters of illogical gun control and had the mentality of a small rock. They shouted down any intelligent conversation or arguments from 2nd amendment supporters. Many of these people supporting gun control were funded by Oprah, George Clooney, Stephen Spielberg, and other big names from the left who gave large donations to fund this radical event. You can see the Anti-Christ manipulating the youth of today. They are using them as pawns.

Youth Demonstrations

I hope that by reading this book, you are seeing a Ribbon of Darkness threading through the mindset of "do gooders'" who are socialist, progressive, liberals, anti-Christ, Anti constitutionalists, and more than willing to take your inalienable rights away from you like David Hogg, and his band of people, and others that I have mentioned. The youth protest against having guns and wanting to get rid of the 1st and 2nd amendment was well schooled at suckering in "useful idiots". They deserve the snow flake award. The people who are actually providing the large amount of money for this purpose are influenced by the communist and socialist parties. They want a One World Order. It simply did not come from the children, but like in Nazi Germany under Hitler the "youthful idiots" were used in a very vicious way to accomplish what Hitler set out to do.

Chapter Thirty-One
Take Action

Have you a desire to be a soldier of God?

We the people are in such a state, that we are willing to grasp at any straw or fragment of hope, and try anything for a change. Just changing politicians will not solve the problem. God has spoken to us, and there are many who have heard His voice. He has given us a clear vision and an answer that rings with a resounding triumph of rejoicing. I truly believe that the answers are in His word and that which I have been sharing with you. But it is up to us! He has called those true leaders to step forward and implement these things! These things mean being proactive at the grassroots level. Don't vote for something unless you completely understand what you are voting for. Question all things on whether <u>God</u> would approve of it. Your gifts from the Holy Spirit have strengthened you so be bold with your gifts and use them. As an example, for the past twelve years many of us have been trying to teach the leadership of the church and nation, God's principles and values through the Constitution. Three of the books used are, "Building of America", "The Five Thousand year Leap," and the Bible, with the Bible by your side; you can become involved by listening to His Word. Yes, it takes a desire but it also takes a determination to make heaven your home, and to keep your freedom and liberties. You cannot call yourself a soldier of God unless you have the willingness to go to battle and fight against evil.

The prophet Micah was a younger contemporary of Isaiah, Amos and Hosea. Things were going well for the people and the people were prospering although there was compromise and corruption everywhere. Micah's name means, "Who is like Yahweh (God)!" His name suited his purpose which was to reveal God. He came to confront sin and declare God's righteous standard. The people were complacent, thinking it is no big deal. Micah said, "Wrong! You don't get it." His words were pungent and personal. God hates sin: He's not casually indifferent, and He will not wink at it. His hatred is real, because of what it does; it destroys. As such, He stands as a righteous judge ready to deal with it. So, too, God's love is just as real, for that is what is motivating His hatred of sin. Judgment will happen if we don't change. Micah then predicts the fall of both Israel and Judah. He knew they didn't get it, and that judgment was going to come, and thus he spoke through the impending doom to a better day. He saw the hope of what will be, because he knew who God was. Judgment comes because of what we do, in order that He might rescue who we are, and so that He might restore us to what we are meant to be. That is a very clear invitation to repent. This is what God wants—let's makes it simple; do justice, love mercy and kindness, and walk humbly with your God. He stands ready, willing, and able to pardon all who repent. He has shown you—now do it!

What does it take to encourage people to share the things that could bring someone to the Lord? Or to share those things that can have a positive effect on our life style? I believe if more of us would share on Social media, their honest feelings and things that others have posted instead of just liking them, or giving thumbs up, more people would see the truth. It may have a positive impact on someone's life!

It's nice that people are starting to realize the movement of God "outside" the church. Amongst those are people who have the heart of willingness to serve and put actions to their words, and are willing to say "never again is now". They truly realize that all lives DO matter. God has given us a clear vision on how He is harvesting the fields. I thank God for those who were involved at all levels at the Birmingham event sponsored by Guiding Light Church and Glenn Beck. Those who participated and are willing to bring those God given applications home with them, realize that they need to be involved right now in applying them. So we see, it takes more than just prayer and waiting upon the Lord, "Gideon's army" is rising up and moving! We must put our prayers into action. <u>Be prepared for more and more persecution</u>! Defeating evil is not easy, as we know, it takes the remnant of God and the righteous amongst us to make a stand and act!

Are we willing to say No, Never Again to evil? Rage and entitlement are things that we <u>must</u> say no to. Saying such things as "we need to be gender neutral", you cannot talk about a particular subject because we are a diverse society.

You must be politically correct at all times, is not biblical. What this means is taking the stand for Jesus Christ. We are going to have to stand, defend, and fight for our constitution! If we let the government take our constitution from us we are done as a free nation. Say goodbye to the western world! We must insist on our freedom of speech! When our freedom of speech is threatened we need to stand up and fight for it even If we have to get a lawyer or go to court, we have to fight these battles! When your Christian walk is being attacked, you must stand up and have a voice and use the constitution! When I was working, someone in my workplace kept taking the Lord's name in vain, so I stood up and made a complaint and reported it to HR. They told me I was the only Christian in the company to ever do that! I heard His name used wrongly all the time at work, and I was the first one to make a formal complaint!

I believe the third great awakening started August 28-29, 2015, in Birmingham, Alabama, with 30,000 people marching, linked arm in arm, because "all lives matter to God"! Iowa and Florida also took part in the freedom works and it has spread throughout this nation! What is the news around your Christian family? We need to be sharing much more than we have been!

We the People need to confront the leadership of our church, and inform them to share and apply our God given constitutional rights. We have been in deception for so many years from the pulpit that we no longer are standing up for what is right and confronting that which is wrong. "The only thing necessary for triumph of evil is for good men to do nothing". That is why the body of Christ is suffering. We the parishioners no longer know how to discipline ourselves, and we are not bringing our children up in the "way of the Lord". David Barton, from Wall builders, has information and explains a number of themes and messages that should be taught from the pulpit such as "How to recognize and change our community, schools, and church for the glory of God." It is worth looking up.

It's time for us, as believers, to be seeking those called by God, in our Spiritual leadership, to teach us about resistance. I have been studying and looking at scripture on this and find that the scripture has a lot to say. Our great warriors from World War 1 and 2, the Civil War, and the war of 1812, prayed and sought scriptures to lead them into battle. There is a lot to be learned by networking with other like-minded groups seeking the same principles and values. Stop believing in the lie that we won't see persecution, or that persecution won't happen in America! Face the truth. We need to organize ourselves and stick together so that we can help each other as tribulation comes our way. Many of you are familiar with the Corrie Tenboom story; I suggest you get the movie, and also the movie, "Return to the Hiding Place" and pay attention to what they are teaching. Watch the Blaze and check out the "Archives." Tribulation is coming to America! We will see persecution. We need to prepare ourselves and be ready for this.

When troubles and hard times come, please know that you are not alone. We understand there is no peace, no serenity, in our lives without Christ Jesus the Savior! He is the One that said "Lowe, I am with you always." This is a promise you can count on. He asked us to be the light unto the world. He will help you shine!

Signs of our broken covenant

We have failed when it comes to educating immigrants for American citizenship. We have failed the youth in our school systems about the true history on how America came into existence. One needs this knowledge to be able to understand the Book of Revelation, with the situation that is happening in the east and why Isis will bring a jihad caliphate to America. This is why it is so critical that the churches who are "serious about the Word of God" make a firm and righteous stand in placing people who seek and desire God's will into office while encouraging the youth who have the wisdom of the Word of God to go into political offices. America, as the House of Israel, will not see true peace again, until the Messiah comes back!

Foundations of America

I believe there are enough Americans out there who would be willing to fight for their liberties and freedom if they could learn how to apply God's Word to their individual lives and to their nation. I am putting this plea out to home groups, and Bible study groups, as well as encouraging this in the churches. My suggestion to get started is to have a good Geneva Bible, or the Founders' Bible by David Barton. Use these along with studying the "5000 year leap" DVD set, and "Building of America", as well as, "Foundations of America". All can be found on Wallbuilders.com All of these books interact and are supported by God's Word. We cannot cure what is ailing America unless we learn our history with God and the Covenant we have with Him and our nation.

It has been my experience that if you take a moral stand on principles and values or claim to be a Christian and follow Christ, the progressives and liberals will oppose you and all of your Christian values! They generally do not have the capability to understand that we are capable of loving them without condoning that which isn't of God. I have been criticized for saying "anyone can go to hell, but not everyone will go to heaven."

The election for the Presidency is well over! We all know this and must move on. This does not mean that we throw in the towel when it comes to political issues and responsibilities as Christians to see that the Bill of Rights and the Constitution are upheld. Right now is the time to double down and teach classes in our churches and home Bible studies on all of these issues. When there is political issues that come up, we have the scripture to rely on and support us. Some examples would be the bathroom policies in North Carolina, and special interest groups as well as taking over the school system with similar common core programs. All of these things just don't undermine the "core" principles of our nation, but also the family and the church. This is why we must stay active in our current events and political issues.

Regarding levies, bonds, and other entitlement programs here is something you probably won't hear from most spiritual leaders. As we know the Bible says "render unto

Caesar that which is Caesar's and to God what is God's"
in Mark 12:17, King James Bible. There are other golden
nuggets on this topic that can be found in God's Word.

One of our country's greatest problems is that we have
not paid heed to God's Word! We have allowed our tax
dollars to feed and exploit anti-Christ policies. You might
ask yourself what some of these things are. The public school
system, Needle exchange programs, same sex homosexual
policies, birth control, abortions etc. Also In the state of
Washington we are allowing our tax dollars to build a
shelter for homeless drug addicts to go and shoot up freely!
These are the hottest issues but when you come to the
knowledge of what co-dependency really means, you will
soon see the total disregard of God's Word! Think before
you vote on any tax entitlement fund raising issue. These
all have consequences. Read Deuteronomy 6:2. This verse is
a promise for long life if you "fear the Lord" and keep His
statues and commandments. It's a promise to all generations.

I read "The Unholy Trinity", a book by Matt Kibbe. I
am very impressed. Matt has really exposed how Satan and
the Anti-Christ movement have destroyed the moral fabric
of America and also the moral principles and values of our
Christian heritage. I highly recommend this book be placed
in every middle and high school. It shows the decay from the
inside out and the cover up by the church. It's very revealing!

While visiting with a friend of mine this weekend, a
topic came up; food for thought: If you were to have a
Face Book page like mine, where you take a biblical and
current event point of view and strip yourself of evangelical
or denominational labels, you just stand firm on the Word

of God, <u>you will be persecuted</u>! Speaking the truth requires wearing the full armor of God. The hardest thing to do in these times is to stand for righteousness and oppose sin. The Lord says we become a new creature in Him when we accept His life style for we forsake our old sinful and immoral ways. 2 Corinthians 5:17, King James: "Therefore if any man *be* in Christ, *he is* a new creature: old things are passed away; behold, all things are become new".

Oh well! My thought is that in America there are many people who do know how to change their life styles and have heard the Word of God. The Bible has always been legal in this nation, as well as free for the asking, yet there will be so many to whom God will say "I knew you not" because they did not take a righteous stand against laws that are opposing His Word. People choose to be in denial over that, but God will hold them accountable for what they did and did not do. That is why I keep marching on in the battle for truth. Support those groups and organizations that are of like mind.

It's my hope that we can make a change where we think it is impossible. If enough of us who believe in the Constitution, the Bill of rights, and the scripture become proactive by using the tools that God has given us in scripture, we can make a difference. It's time that we stop hiding behind the defeatist attitude that "it won't do any good". That attitude never succeeded in anything. It's time that we replace liberals and progressives with like-minded people who believe in the American dream. Encourage others to be responsible Americans.

Where has the sacredness gone?

I would like to bring to your attention these militant thugs called "protesters"! We were founded on Christian –Judeo values and when we weaken that by taking God and Christ out of our system we are asking exactly for this kind of behavior. I refer you to Exodus 22. What do you think we Christ followers should do about this? What do you do?

True followers of God and His word, believe that politics <u>do</u> have a place in the pulpit.

Evangelist Eric Love from Georgia

As a brother in Christ, I know that attacks against Christianity and moral values are the raging war that has broken America's covenant. They are not isolated cases, but have become pretty much the "norm". If you are a minister of God's Word and, wish to apply for permits to evangelize on the public streets, during a gay pride festival see how far you can get! If you want to fly the Christian flag in prominent places such as the "rainbow flag" is flown on top of the Space needle in downtown Seattle, see how far you will get! To tell you the truth, I am more disgusted at those who call themselves Christians and say "yah, but" and do not have the willingness to stand for the truth. It is not just the cake or the flowers at the florist, it is not just passing the legislation to muzzle the Word of God publically, but it is the denial of who our savior is! This shows us why our nation is in such an upheaval because no one is willing to fight for their moral inalienable rights and principles. I question the true salvation of those who are willing to do nothing and continue to make excuses and belittle these serious issues. Matthew 12:36, NIV, [36] "But I tell you that everyone will have to give account on the Day of Judgment for every empty word they have spoken".

I have been asked by some, "what is the unpardonable sin"? The unpardonable sin is committed by people who resist the work of the Holy Spirit and reject His witness concerning Jesus.

James 1:26 (NKJV), [26] "If anyone among you thinks he is religious, and does not bridle his tongue but deceives his own heart, this one's religion *is* useless".

Read James 1:21-27. The word gives us spiritual birth. It is like seed planted in the heart that produces spiritual fruit. It is a mirror that helps us examine ourselves and cleanse our lives. We must do the Word of God, not just read or study it; the blessing is in the doing. If you speculate on truth and do not do it, it is worthless. Truth is given to be done not contemplated!

We are a lost nation. We have lost our identity! Many people like me have been sounding the alarm for many years now. There have been times throughout the years, when I and many others have wanted to throw the towel in and give up because of people's apathy and unwillingness to change. However the pendulum is swinging the other direction now and our prayers are being answered. By the spirit of God moving, people are coming back to their God given principles and values. Through this we can be the difference in cleaning out the corruption in our nation from our towns and cities all the way to the White House. The Spirit of God is showing the people that it has to start at home and spread from there. Only we can put a stop to what's happening in schools. Stop unisex bathrooms and other sexual immoralities being taught as normal behavior. We the people are the only ones who can put a stop to the slaughtering of unborn children, and beheading Christians and the evil killing of our police officers and the corruption that is going on in the military. We need to do this by taking a stand! We need to be God's hands and feet! We need to get off our butts, get on our knees, and do His work!

Chapter Thirty-Two
The Alarm

Who is sounding the alarm?

I find it quite interesting as I look into the social media at the different topics. I see the games that people play so they are not being offensive to anyone. I have observed that the people, who pretend to be more spiritual or religious, stick to Sunday school picnics, games and shows. In other words, the cruise ship mentality. The majority of the people who have a large following in sounding the alarm are those that we don't look at as personal friends or spiritual leaders, but in reality they are.

It is people like you who stand up for principles, values and integrity. They will not compromise to please the carnal ways of man. They take the truth seriously in everything that they are involved in. You do this at a cost and your Heavenly Father knows that. It may cost relationships, it may draw slander, and it may cost you by going to prison, or even take your life! Yet you are willing to stand shoulder to shoulder with those people of like minds in the word of truth.

I want to encourage all my friends not to let the stress

and anger of the political season get you down and ruin your life. Every day I look at my Facebook and I notice where I have lost one or two friends. I find it upsetting because my goal is to enlighten people and encourage them to have a better life knowing God is the answer for the world today. We would have stronger families and personal relationships with one another if we focus on what is good and what is true. He is the only truth and the only one who has all the answers. I don't, and no one does, except the Lord! A big THANK YOU to all of you out there for your friendships!

Do not get too discouraged over the events of our times. There will always be those who cannot be reached or cannot understand because they do not read the Bible faithfully and do not ponder what God is saying and applying it to their lives. However we can praise Him through all things and shout that we have the victory when all is said and done.

About the Author

The day after I had to put Tangier, my beloved guide dog down, my Aunt Eva passed away. It was not a shock or surprise as she had been ailing from cancer for some time. What is interesting is that she led worship services at the little country church in Ellensburg WA, Pastor Gob's Tabernacle Church. She had a clear, clean, sweet voice that you could hear for a country mile! She would win the "leather lung" award for sure! She and Grandma Black hair, who was her mother, and my Grandma White hair, my Dad's mother, were the prayer warriors to claim my soul for Christ. Grandma Black hair and my Aunt Eva stuck the "Hound Dog of Heaven", (Holy Spirit) on me.

I was the furthest thing from being a perfect child! I grew up to be a recovering alcoholic and drug addict and God had to cleanse my mouth and my brain from foul language and jokes. Then he had to turn around and heal a bitter, black, broken, hardened and angered heart. He had to take me from death's door more than once.

Matthew 10:14, NIV, "if anyone will not welcome you or listen to your words, leave that home or town and shake the dust off your feet." Matthew 10:14 can be a misunderstood scripture. We all have heard you can lead a horse to water, but you can't make him drink it. I am saying here that we can serve the bread of life and God's Word at the banquet table and alter of love, however we cannot force someone to participate and feast upon the bread of life. I count myself fortunate that there were people who believed in Jesus Christ and the Holy Spirit who persevered and the Holy Spirit caused me to realize that there was something that had to be changed in my life. This meant that I had to be bold enough to make permanent changes with whom I hung out and participated with in life. It wasn't what was said by a phony Christian but it was the word of God that the Holy Spirit brought through people's actions and words that were honest that caused me to have the desire and it made me hungry for God's word and made me want to be a Christian and live for Christ.

After all these years of being on Face Book, "social media", I have been faithful to make a stand for Christ and the true heritage of our nation. I have taken note of the people who have "unfriended" me because of my principles and values, and their lack of understanding; but I will always be praying that God through the Holy Spirit will guide them to the truth and that they will be anchored there within God's Word.

A Rev. Mel Jolley quote:

"Is history being written, or was history written and is just now being fulfilled? The answer is in the Word of God."

Mel's Psalm 1

For my heart has been whipped. And my soul has been bruised. And my spirit has been broken. Oh Lord how I thirst for the water that springs from your throne. And how I hunger for the banquet of your daily bread that is portioned out to me! How I long for your serenity and your peace. For I have not seen these until I can see your light glowing from within me. Let me feel the burning of your spirit through the marrows of my bone. Let me sleep in thy bosom while you comfort me the days of my life. How I repent of my uncleanliness and your righteousness astounds me for its purity and fairness. How I hunger to gaze upon your face and feel the comfort of your hand guiding me in your ways and not those of mine. You are more than just a friend. You are more than just a morning star, and the dew that is on the lilies. Master how I bow before you and desire to serve you. Keep me safe and in your bosom until you take me home with you.

Written by Rev. Mel Jolley
Thank you for reading this book!

Rev Mel Jolley
Go Forth Ministries
Contact me through my publisher.